Feeding
Wild Birds
in Winter

Feeding Wild

CLIVE DOBSON

Birds in Winter

FIREFLY BOOKS

Firefly Books Ltd.
3520 Pharmacy Avenue, Unit 1-C
Scarborough, Ontario. M1W 2T8

Printed in Canada

ISBN 0-920668-17-8

Contents

Acknowledgements

Many thanks to Lionel Koffler for the idea, Nori Nakashima for the advice and patience, Wayne Kelosky and Mark Thurman for illustration assistance, Kathy Vanderlinden for editing, and Ma and Pa who started feeding birds long before I even cared.

Each new year is a surprise to us. We find that we had virtually forgotten the note of each bird, and when we hear it again it is remembered like a dream, reminding us of a previous state of existence.

How happens it that the associations it awakens are always pleasing, never saddening; reminiscences of our sunniest hours? The voice of nature is always encouraging.

H. THOREAU, WALDEN

1

Getting Started:
A Simple Program

A streak of red in a snow-covered landscape. A pair of cardinals comes to rest on the raised feeder just a few feet from the kitchen window. They're back again this cold morning to peck up the sunflower seeds spread out in anticipation of their arrival.

Such a gratifying spectacle is the reward of simple feeding programs that many people have set up to help birds weather the winter months. The popularity of winter feeding is fortunate, for without it many birds would be unable to sustain themselves in the snow-covered latitudes of this continent. More than ever birds have come to rely on the consistent supply of food offered to them in our gardens.

Establishing a feeding program is inexpensive and with common sense can be a simple matter. It is possible to turn your yard into a circus with all the gizmos and contraptions available on the market today, but a yard, some feed, a few feeders and patience are all that are actually necessary.

Although this book deals primarily with feeding in winter —the most crucial time, since birds can find natural sources the rest of the year—one should also consider year-round feeding. Attracting wild birds to your yard during the warmer seasons can do wonders for the garden. A small local bird population can control weeds and insects better than any single-purpose chemical. Birds present no environmental hazards, rather an environmental enhancement.

After a winter season of caring for a few hungry birds, you may even find them appreciative enough in the spring to raise their young in one of your trees.

The first snow always takes us a little by surprise. To see the ground so completely covered makes us wonder how all the birds and animals are going to find food. This is when you should be getting a regular feeding program underway.

Mid-fall, in fact, is probably the last date you should plan to begin putting out food, for it will help birds get acquainted with your feeding grounds. They will then be more likely to include you in their feeding territory as soon as the weather turns cold and snowy.

If you are undertaking a bird-feeding program for the first time, there are a number of immediate steps you can take:

1. Find some stale bread (new bread is O.K. too), crackers, breakfast cereal, raisins, nuts, seeds or popcorn.
2. Outside your favorite viewing window scatter one or a

combination of these easily-found kitchen items in a six-foot-square clearing or packed down area you have made in the snow. If you haven't the use of a yard, a sheltered rooftop or windowsill may have to do. You can also use the tops of picnic tables, or stumps. Some birds prefer a perch. Instructions for constructing a few simple feeders are given in chapter 4.

3. Observe. For a better understanding of what is actually taking place before you, I would strongly recommend obtaining a pair of binoculars.

Be patient. It takes some time for local birds to find that there is a new feeding ground available to them.

Once your feeding area is attracting birds on a regular basis, your program can become more sophisticated. You may wish to try special types of feed to attract particular birds, or build more elaborate feeders, or transform your entire garden into a habitat for birds. It is almost certain that you will develop an increasing interest in and appreciation of birds and birdlife.

The chapters that follow offer the basics for setting up a simple, or a more complex, winter feeding program: birds—their appearance and behavior; food; feeders; habitat; problems and solutions.

Areas of average minimum winter temperatures (Celsius)

1	-40° to -50°
2	-30° to -40°
3	-20° to -30°
4	-10° to -20°
5	0° to -10°
6	10° to 0°

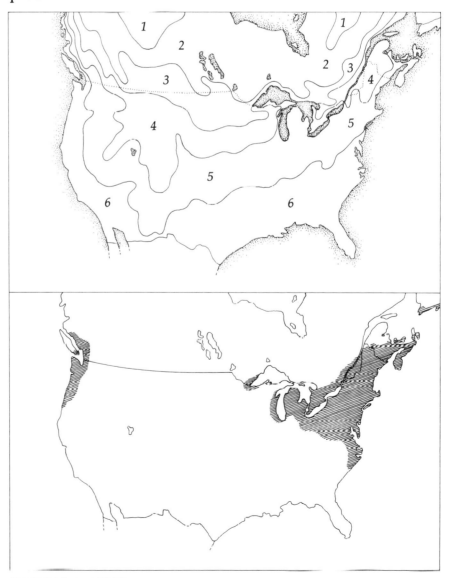

Shaded portions indicate major areas where winter feeding has altered the migration pattern of many species of birds.

2 The Winter Birds

There are approximately fifty species of birds mentioned in this chapter that can be fed or assisted in some way in the winter. This is a small proportion of the recorded total of about 750 species that spend at least part of the year on this continent. The number of birds that winter in snow-covered areas has increased dramatically in recent years. Many species are unlikely to arrive at your feeding station, however, as their independent nature keeps them for the most part away from human civilization: hawks and owls are good. examples.

Even within the limited number of species with which North Americans are well acquainted can be found incredible variety in form and behavior. Comparing a Pileated Woodpecker with a Winter Wren will give some idea.

Observation of these birds at close range can give us a more realistic perspective of all living things. It is not just the birds themselves that we observe, but their part in the world and their contribution to the whole.

Blackbirds Common Grackle

Winter Range: Southern parts of great lakes to Florida, inland to central states.

Habitat: Farm fields, towns, shrubbery, feeding normally at the ground level.

Description: **Males** — 13". Iridescent black coloring, no light markings other than the purple-blue, green and bronze shimmers about the **head and shoulders. Females** — Slightly smaller, more brown in coloring.

Common Grackle

Grackles have slowly increased their numbers over the last decade and have shifted their migration patterns, now staying further north during the winter months. These large blackbirds are common visitors to feeders as far north as New Hampshire, Vermont and southern Ontario. They are well adapted to the human environment where they are often seen scrounging discarded bread and such wastes of our fast food stands in parks and roadside picnic areas. Normally Grackles prefer feeding at the ground level where they are well supported with their large and agile feet. Rather than hop about like Robins they walk placing one foot well ahead of the other, weaving back and forth as they go. Their long, broad tail serves as a further balance. Feeding Grackles is a simple matter — they will eat almost anything. Sometimes flocks of these birds make feeding difficult for some of the other, smaller birds.

When their presence becomes a problem, you may have to reduce ground feeding and restrict the amount of bread and kitchen scraps you are putting out. If food is scarce, you can expect to see them at feeders consuming anything you have left. Sometimes Grackles can be rather nasty to other birds, and you may find it necessary to provide bread or stale baked goods for them in a separate location. These birds are capable of carrying off large pieces of food at one time owing to the size of their bills. Grackles have adapted so well to the rapid changes that this continent is undergoing that we can expect them to be with us forever.

Red-winged Blackbird

Winter Range: Previously restricted to southern states and West Indies, winter range seems to be expanding further north up Mississippi River as far as Great Lakes and up eastern seaboard as far as southern tip of Nova Scotia.

Habitat: Open marshy areas, fields, areas of scrubby lowlands, pastures.

Description: 9″. Males — Solid black with visible red patch on shoulder plus small band of yellow. Females — brownish, mottled dark stripings.

Normally this bird's presence is synonymous with spring. Although wary of humans, Red-winged Blackbirds have started visiting feeders more frequently during periods when food is scarce. Like the Common Grackle, Redwings will eat almost anything normally fed other birds. If these birds visit your feeder, they will come in large flocks and stay for only a short period of time. Expect to see more of this presently adapting bird in the years to come.

Brown-headed Cowbird
Common Cowbird

Winter Range: Same as Red-winged Blackbird with a slightly extended northern range.

Habitat: Wood edges, river groves, roadsides farmlands.

Description: Male — 7″. Black body with brown head. *Female —* Warm gray, identified by finchlike bill. Male and female smaller than either Red-winged Blackbird or Common Grackle.

The cowbird is easily distinguished by the upright tail displayed when ground feeding. Like the Red-winged Blackbird they usually travel in flocks, preferring to feed at ground level and occasionally at feeders.

Visits in winter are not as common as in the warmer seasons, since some of these birds migrate as far south as northern Mexico. After laying her eggs in the spring the female deposits them in the nests of other birds, where the offspring are reared by a foster parent.

Creepers

Brown Creeper

Winter Range: Alaska, Canada to Nicaragua, predominantly in forest regions of northeast. Most birds leave extreme northern latitudes in winter.

Habitat: Wooded areas.

Description: 5". Separated stiff tail and fine curved bill. Well camouflaged by its mottled gray-brown back with white underside.

These small birds are hard to spot because of their bark-like coloring and feather pattern. But they can be easily recognized by their characteristic upward spiral movement when climbing trees to search for tiny insects. The stiff tail is used as a brace during the ascent. Peanut butter or suet smeared on tree trunks will be readily accepted by these birds. A vertically positioned suet log will also attract Brown Creepers.

Finches

Snow Bunting

Winter Range: Moving down from arctic to central North America no further than mid-states prairie regions.

Habitat: Prairies, open farmlands, areas of no cover or little vegetation.

Description: 7". White in summer with black back and wing tips. Underside almost entirely white. **In winter white areas change to** warmer ochre colors and black back to mottled brown.

Unlike most birds the Snow Bunting prefers to feed in the open at ground level where it can find smaller seeds. These birds are acclimatized to the cold. In the summer months they prefer the northerly arctic tundra regions where their range extends completely around the globe. Snow Buntings travel great distances in flocks in their daily search for food. Scattered seed of almost any grain on top of the snow will attract these birds as long as there is plenty of open space. The Snow Bunting is one of the few birds hardy enough to take the cruel prairie winters.

Cardinal (Northern)

Winter Range: From south half of Great Lakes, New England states south to Mexico, inland as far as central states.

Habitat: Wooded lots, forest edges, town garden areas — where there is a mixture of shrubs and trees.

Description: 9″. Males — **Solid red** with darker red on back, wings and tail. Bright red crest, red bill, **black face mask. Female** — Olive-colored with red highlights on wings, crest, tail and beak. Same mask as male. Both have large, thick bills, appropriate for cracking the hulls of seeds.

The Cardinal is perhaps the brightest-colored of all the birds one might expect in the winter. This bird has adapted well to the treed areas of cities and towns, where it makes itself at home eating almost anything, but especially sunflower seeds from our feeders. Its northern range is extending further and further north in the winter months in response to the popularity of winter feeding. Cardinals do not travel in large numbers but rather in pairs or small groups. They will take food from feeding tables, raised feeders and ground areas.

Red Crossbill

Winter Range: James Bay to upper half of Great Lakes, Newfoundland to Great Slave Lake, irregularly south to lower states.

Habitat: Coniferous forest regions.

Description: Male — 6″. Dull red with darker brownish-black wings and tail. Female — Olive-gray with darker brownish-black wings and tail. Both have crossed mandibles (see illustration).

Head portion of Red Crossbill showing peculiar crossed mandibles which allow this specialized species to remove seeds easily from various evergreen cones.

White-winged Crossbill

Winter Range: Similar to Red Crossbill. Northern range extended to top of Labrador — even more scarce south of Great Lakes.

Habitat: Coniferous forest regions.

Description: Same size as Red Crossbill (6"), same crossed mandibles. Male — Lighter red to pink. Two white bands on darker black wings. Female — Similar to female Red Crossbill but with two white bands on wings.

The crossbills are not the most common sight at feeding stations, probably because of their extremely specialized feeding habits. Their natural diet consists almost entirely of the cone seeds of spruce, hemlock, fir and some pine, which they easily extract with their sharp, crossed bills. The heavily treed coniferous forests of the far north (as far north as the tundra regions) are the most suitable areas for these birds. Occasionally they will eat sunflower seeds and other smaller grain seeds from feeders.

Purple Finch

Winter Range: Pacific coastal forests, Great Lakes south to Florida and Texas, northeastern states and Nova Scotia.

Habitat: Wooded areas, forest edges, towns, shrubbery.

Description: Male — 5½". Pinkish-red, brightest on head rump and upper chest. Tail and wings brown with pinkish highlights on feathers. Female — No evidence of pink coloring. Darker brown wings and tail, mottled chest stripes, darker patch near eye and throat.

The Purple Finch is quite a common winter guest. If not for the pink coloring of the males, a flock of these birds could easily be mistaken for sparrows. For their size they have fairly large bills suited to cracking open sunflower seeds. Sometimes these birds are mistaken for the introduced House Finch, a bird with similar markings that has been rapidly multiplying since its 1940 introduction. The male House Finch has a more vermillion coloring with a prominent red slash above the eye. The female is similar to the Purple Finch but generally lighter in color. The House Finch is restricted at present to the eastern states and lower Great Lakes.

Both species will eat masses of sunflower seeds, taking other seeds only as second choice.

Evening Grosbeak

Winter Range: Newfoundland to Florida, irregular migration south to Texas, from Florida west across prairies to Mexico.

Habitat: Coniferous forests, suburban treed areas, shrubs, fruit trees.

Description: Male — Dirty yellow body, black tail and wings with prominent white patch, darker head with yellow forehead and eye slash, pale yellow-green beak. Female — Faded version of male less head markings. Gray-olive color, white markings on wings apparent. Both have short tails and are larger than usual for finches — approx. 8".

Evening Grosbeak

The arrival of a flock of Evening Grosbeaks will come as a surprise, for their migration habits are extremely irregular. When these birds fly in, practically all other birds will be displaced by and at the mercy of these greedy hordes. The mass consumption of sunflower seeds is almost unbelievable. Taking one seed at a time, they quickly crack it, shells falling to the sides, swallow the kernel and take up the next seed all in one motion. After a flock has emptied your feeders, only a giant pile of shells will remain. These birds are so messy and greedy that large amounts of uncracked seeds are usually mixed with the shells and appropriately left for other, slower ground-feeding species to sort out.

Pine Grosbeak

Winter Range: Newfoundland west through upper St. Lawrence to northern parts of Great Lakes, spruce belt westward.

Habitat: Coniferous forests, wooded areas.

Description: Larger-sized finch — approx. 9." Longer tail, small head, stubby, slightly hooked bill. Male — dirty rose color, darker slate-colored wings, two noticeable white bands on wings, dark slate-colored tail. Female — same as male only red coloring absent. Olive-gray on most of body, same wing and tail coloring.

Pine Grosbeaks stay further north in the winter than most of the other finches. When winters are extremely harsh or food supplies scarce, there seems to be a more southerly invasion. Appropriate cultivated vegetation will attract these birds as well as any feed you might put out. Pine Grosbeaks are attracted to berry-producing shrubs, orchards, garden plants that may have remaining fruits or seeds. Once these birds realize that food is available at your feeders, they will prefer ground feeding on currants, sunflower seeds, cranberries, apples. Pine Grosbeaks are extremely tame birds—your presence outside will be easily tolerated. Try hand feeding.

Northern Junco
Slate-colored Junco
Oregon Junco
White-winged Junco

Winter Range: Eastern version or **Slate-colored** — **Great Lakes, Newfoundland** to southern states. Western version or Oregon — **Alaska, Western Canada, south Pacific states.** White-winged — **Black Hills of South Dakota.**

Habitat: Mixed coniferous and decidious forests, forest edges, shrubbery.

Description: 6". Male — Slate gray color with white stomach and obvious outer white tail feathers. Western version — more brown apparent on white stomach area, brown coloring on back. White-winged variety has white wing markings. Female — Same as male only slightly paler.

Slate-colored Junco

The Northern Junco is easily identified in flight by the white feathers on the outside of the tail.

Juncos of any variety happening to frequent your area are quiet, ground-feeding birds that appear in flocks whenever the weather turns for the worse. These birds are very economical to feed, for they clean up any spilled seeds from feeders. Ground tables and stump tops are also suitable feeding areas. Most often these birds like to feed in open ground areas as long as there are nearby shrubs or trees for cover. All Juncos have the same ground-foraging habits. When winter strikes the west coast regions, you can count on having these birds around through the entire period that snow covers the ground.

Common Redpoll
Hoary Redpoll

Winter Range: Irregular winter migration from James Bay south to mid-states.

Habitat: Boreal forests, tundra, shrub areas, brush, weeds.

Description: Small, sparrow-sized bird (5"), gray-brown streaks on back and sides, red cap, black throat patch. Male has light pink chest. The Hoary Redpoll has more white in chest and rump areas.

Redpolls are birds that breed in the far north, coastal Greenland, Baffin Island and areas of Hudson's Bay. In the winter there is an erratic southerly migration of the Common Redpoll to the northern states. Food scarcity may cause them to move further and further south, but they are rare at backyard feeding stations. Relying heavily on natural weed seeds in the winter, these birds may appear in flocks when exceptionally harsh winters hit the northern regions and snow covers most of the lower weed vegetation. Hoary Redpolls are very rare at feeders, for their winter range is limited to regions of their arctic breeding grounds, and they only move south in extremely severe winters to the northern parts of the Great Lakes. All redpolls are quite tame in the presence of man. Their diet at feeders includes sunflower seeds, small grain seeds and suet.

Pine Siskin

Winter Range: Southern Canada, **upper New England states,** Newfoundland. South irregularly to southernmost states, Mexico.

Habitat: Coniferous and deciduous forests weeds, scrub brush.

Description: 4½". Heavily-striped, dull-brown male has yellow touches on wings, rump and tail areas. Wings and tail slightly darker than rest of striped body areas.

A very familiar sight at feeding stations are flocks of these birds. When they arrive, you may find that some of the other birds will be intimidated by these tiny finches and will have to leave. Their small, sharp bills are functional for extruding small seeds from weed plants and cones. At feeding stations these birds will pick at empty sunflower shells, taking any small pieces other birds have overlooked. Scratch feed, millet and suet appeal to Pine Siskins. Like the redpoll these birds can become quite tame. They are easily taught to take small seeds from the hand. Their streamlined bodies and small size allows them to feed at any kind of feeder.

Fox Sparrow

Winter Range: Southern Ontario, New England states to Gulf of Mexico.

Habitat: Lower levels of forests, underbrush, overgrown swamp areas, leaves.

Description: 7". The most rusty-brown colored of the sparrows. Tail is a solid rust-brown, chest white with heavy rust flecks. Distinguished from other sparrows by its larger size and brighter color.

Although most of these birds head south in winter to wooded areas of the southeastern states, growing numbers are staying in the northern limits of the range and becoming more dependent on feeding stations. They are predominantly ground feeding and make use of their oversized feet to scratch about in dead leaves in search of food. After a snowfall Fox Sparrows will root about until they have exposed the ground where they can find seeds. They will take millet, scratch food, suet and sunflower seeds from feeding stations at the ground level. These birds tend to be very shy.

American Tree Sparrow

Winter Range: Central North America, northern states, southern tip of Canada — southern Ontario, New Brunswick, Nova Scotia.

Habitat: Underbrush, forest edges, exposed weed fields, swamp scrub.

Description: 6". Identified by a single dark patch on lighter chest area. Head has a rust-brown cap. Upper mandible is dark gray, lower mandible yellow.

The American Tree Sparrow can take cold weather much more easily than the other sparrows. These birds, like juncos, will appear in small groups when the weather has turned cold. Unlike the Fox Sparrow they are just as suited to perching while feeding as to feeding on the ground. Their diet is mainly small seeds. Substitute millet, sunflower, hemp, buckwheat or wheat when the weather makes wild food inaccessible. The Tree Sparrow is also capable of taking suet from hanging log feeders. Look for the bicolored bill and chest mark for positive identification.

Rufous-sided Towhee

Winter Range: Eastern strain — Cape Cod south to Florida, Lake Erie to Louisiana. Western strain — coastal areas of British Columbia south to United States.

Habitat: Underbrush, forest floors, forest edges.

Description: 8". Male — Black head, throat, back, wings, tail. White and rust stomach. White markings on tail tips and wings. Female — Dark brown rather than black areas. Western race has more white flecks on wings.

Rufous-sided Towhee

This bird is easily identified by its behavior in wooded areas where it endlessly roots through the leaves in thickets and underbrush. These birds prefer to feed on the ground owing to their well-developed feet suited to uncovering hidden seeds. Towhees are shy birds and will retire to the woods when threatened. Their diet consists mainly of wild seeds, but they will take sunflower seeds, wheat, bread, oats, melon seeds, pumpkin seeds and scratch feed from feeding stations. Their broad fan tail helps stabilize them while feeding.

Grouse

Ruffed Grouse

Winter Range: Labrador south to Alabama, Great Lakes to James Bay, northern areas of Manitoba and Saskatchewan, Alaska, Yukon, British Columbia. Recently introduced to Newfoundland.

Habitat: Ground level of underbrush, forest edges, fields with higher growth for cover, mixed coniferous and deciduous forests.

Description: 19". A large, fowl-like bird with a small crested head, plump body, fantail when flying. Mottled gray head, wings and body, rust-colored tail with a large black band and thin white band. Rust color absent in gray phase.

Grouse are very shy birds and rightly so, since so many of them are shot during the fall hunting season. Feeding Ruffed Grouse in close proximity to buildings will not work. In order to feed these birds you will have to leave buckwheat, cracked corn, wheat, barley or other grains along isolated wood edges or brush protected fence areas near a wood lot. Do not attempt to feed these birds during the fall hunting season as you may only be luring them to needless death.

Jays, Crows   Common Crow

Winter Range: Limited to southern tips of Canada and most of United States.

Habitat: Farmlands, fields, woods, garbage dumps, roadsides, shores.

Description: 20". Solid black, large bills, ragged wing tips in flight.

The snow is so deep and the cold so intense that the crows are compelled to be very bold in seeking out their food and come very near the houses in the village.
H. THOREAU, WALDEN

Common Crow

Crows behave in much the same way today as when *Walden* was written. They will quietly invade feeding grounds in the early morning when heavy winter snows have made natural food supplies scarce. If there are any signs of human activity they will take to the trees, waiting for a better opportunity. Only in certain urban environments (parks, ferry terminals, garbage dumps) will crows tolerate our presence. They are extremely crafty, intelligent birds and have become very versatile in behavior. This versatility has almost ensured their survival, even against the greatest odds. Raiding picnic tables and scavenging dead animals from roadsides and highways are some of their tactics. I once found it necessary to chase one out of the back of my truck after it had discovered a bag of dog meal unattended.

Crows will not usually bother with feeding stations in better weather unless quantities of kitchen scraps or protein matter are made available to them. Garbage dumps will usually provide most of the delicacies suitable to their varied menu.

When the weather turns, you might like to provide some dog meal, bread or kitchen scraps in an isolated location (woods edge) to make things a little easier for these resourceful black marauders.

Black-billed Magpie

Winter Range: Western half of North America.

Habitat: Foothills, sage brush country, dryer coniferous areas near rivers, lakes.

Description: 20". Black and iridescent green with large white wing patch and white stomach. Green most evident on wings and long tail. Prominent black bills.

Black-billed Magpie

This bird is easy to identify at first sight by the large, swooping areas of black and white. The cool green iridescence is quite visible in the sunlight. Their skulking behavior and raucous voices are typical of most members of the family. With the resourcefulness of crows, they scavenge food at any opportunity.

Magpies can become very tame. They will eat almost anything.

Blue Jay

Winter Range: Year-round presence in most of the populated areas of North America east of the Rockies.

Habitat: Wooded areas of mixed coniferous and deciduous trees, oaks, gardens.

Description: 12". Bright cobalt **blue crested bird with gray-white** underside, black necklace band, black and white flecks on wing feathers, black flecks on tail, white-tipped tail feathers.

Blue Jay

Although Blue Jays migrate south in the fall, many stay behind relying on garden feeders to help them through the winter. They are bound to be your loudest guests, for their **call sounds like an accusing "Thief! Thief!" Blue Jays are very** successful at bullying other birds and will maintain possession of a feeder until satisfied. If you have oak trees on your property, you probably already know this bird. Acorns are a favorite food. Blue Jays will eat almost anything, but they prefer corn, peanut hearts, peanuts and sunflower seeds.

Blue Jays visit feeders in small numbers, staying briefly, then disappearing for long periods of time, probably in search of other natural foods. Once they know where to find **your feeders, they will inevitably come back.**

Canada Jay (Gray Jay)

Winter Range: Northern New Englands states, most of Canada east of Rockies.

Habitat: Northern woods, coniferous forests, camp grounds.

Description: Slate-gray back and tail, black patch on back of head, **white forehead and throat, turning** gray on stomach areas, white whiskers.

These birds are inhabitants of boreal forest areas or forests of the Canadian Shield. They are a familiar sight around lumber camps, northern provincial parks and resort areas. They will eat almost anything normally consumed by humans and can become quite bold in our presence. Small quantities of kitchen scraps will appeal to them. Leaving unattended food outside is an open invitation for these quiet opportunists.

Steller's Jay

Winter Range: Northwest coast and mountains.

Habitat: Forest regions of Pacific coast, fir, hemlock, cedars.

Description: Similar to Blue Jay but with charcoal head and shoulders blending into deep blue-colored body and tail. Head has black crest.

The Steller's Jay is one of the most colorful birds of the western forests. Their behavior is similar to that of the Blue Jay although not quite as raucous. Coming to feeders after heavy snowfalls they will stay only long enough to take their share. Typical of jays, Steller's Jays when new to a feeding ground will quietly lurk in nearby trees until they have thoroughly examined the situation at hand. They will eat almost anything you provide, but their favorite foods are sunflower seeds, corn and bread.

Kinglets

Golden-crowned Kinglet

Winter Range: Newfoundland, New Brunswick, Nova Scotia, Great Lakes, most of west coast United States.

Habitat: Cool coniferous forests, hemlock, fir, pine, spruce.

Description: 4". Olive-gray body, black and white markings on wings, small bills. Male — Head has yellow-bordered red cap outlined with black stripe, black line through eye. Female — Similar, but has yellow on cap, no red.

The Golden-crown Kinglet is a small, independent bird that rarely stops long at feeders. They are experts at finding small edible insects that may occur on evergreens. Their movements are fast and erratic with a constant flicking of the wings. They will eat suet from suet log feeders.

Ruby-crowned Kinglet

Winter Range: Areas south of Great Lakes, eastern coast New England to Florida, Pacific coast west of Rockies. Migrates in winter further south than Golden-crowned.

Description: 4" Olive-gray body, black and white markings on wing. Male — Red patch on head. Female — No head markings.

Ruby-crowned Kinglet

The Ruby-crowned Kinglet is more likely to appear at feeders than the Golden-crowned Kinglet, especially in warmer climates. They are not as hardy as the Golden-crowned and will take suet and small seeds from feeders. In northern latitudes they are a common sight in the summer months.

Nuthatches

White-breasted Nuthatch

Winter Range: Northeastern and northwestern states, southern and west coast Canada.

Habitat: Tree trunks, forests wood lots, groves, treed garden areas.

Description: 5″. All nuthatches have plump bodies, short, stubby tails, long, streamlined bills. Pale blue-gray with white underside. Male — Black head and black half-collar around back of neck. Female — Black collar around back of neck, blue-gray cap.

White-breasted Nuthatch

Nuthatches characteristically search the bark of trees, descending the trunk head first. They have strong woodpecker-like bills appropriate for pecking out insects and larvae. Their familiar nasal note heralds their arrival at our feeders. Because of their expert climbing abilities they can easily feed from any kind of feeder, perferably on suet and sunflower seeds. Pasting suet in the rough bark of trees will provide a more natural feeding circumstance for nuthatches. The White-breasted Nuthatch is as familiar a sight as the chickadee at feeding grounds, both in the east and west.

Red-breasted Nuthatch

Winter Range: More northerly range than White-breasted with heavier withdrawal some years from the north. Canadian Shield areas to southern states. West coast.

Habitat: Coniferous forests, mixed forests.

The Red-breasted Nuthatch is not as common as the White-breasted. Behavior and diet of the two varieties is similar.

Pigeons, Doves

Mourning Dove

Winter Range: Great Lakes, southern points of Canada, most of United States.

Habitat: Roadsides, farmlands, open ground, scrub areas.

Description: Warm-gray bird with pointed tail, warmer tones on chest, back and stomach, white tips on tail feathers.

The Mourning Dove's call is as forlorn and eerie as its name suggests. They are primarily ground-feeding birds with a diet of seeds, grain, insects and berries. Mourning Doves are mainly vegetarian and for that reason require a certain amount of grit in their diet. These birds are a familiar sight along gravel roadsides bordering cornfields and other grain crops. At feeding stations they will eat large quantities of grain (corn, wheat, buckwheat, millet). This dove's ability to adapt may save it from the fate of its extinct relative the Passenger Pigeon. Its northern range is increasing year by year.

Band-tailed Pigeon

Winter Range: Moderate Pacific coast regions.

Habitat: Berry-producing trees, scrub areas, roadsides, fields, farms.

Description: 12". Typical pigeon shape, brown chest and head, slight iridescence on back of neck, darker wings, darker band evident on fan-shaped tail.

The Band-tailed Pigeon is a larger member of the family *Columbidae.* They are frequently heard flapping and thrashing about in trees where they are feeding on berries. Although more timid than the eastern Mourning Dove, they will appear at feeders to eat their fill of grain and seeds, especially after a snowfall. The moderate winter climate of the west coast makes the search for food much easier than in the east. These birds are attracted to holly bushes, Arbutus and Gary Oak for the fruit they bear.

Quail, Pheasants

Common Bobwhite

Winter Range: Southern states. Northern limits — Cape Cod, Lake Erie, Minnesota.

Habitat: Wood edges, farmlands, scrub, roadsides.

Description: Mottled brown, fat, fowl-like bird, short tail — fanned when in flight. Lighter underside, darker eye patch, lighter throat.

The Bobwhite is not a bird you can expect to come to your feeding station in the manner of other birds. However, you may catch glimpses of them if you try leaving corn and other grains in a sheltered area away from buildings. Fence lines and forest edge cover are suitable areas to erect some sort of ground level leanto which may attract some Bobwhites after a snowfall. Your binoculars may help in viewing birds like the Bobwhite and pheasant.

Ring-necked Pheasant

Winter Range: More moderate regions of east coast as far north as Nova Scotia. Great Lakes, prairies. Introduced into populated areas of west coast.

Habitat: Farmlands, brush, fields, scrub, fence lines.

Description: 33". All have long, sweeping tails, small heads, plump bodies, extended necks. Male — Multi-colored head, red wattles, iridescent neck with white band. Female — Mottled beige and brown.

Ring-necked Pheasant

Many pheasants are shot for sport in the fall hunting season. They are considered to be one of the finest game birds and are raised domestically on some farms.

In the wild, pheasants have become extremely cautious birds. It is unlikely that they will be seen close to buildings. When feeding pheasants, attract them to areas where hunting is restricted. They will eat corn on the cob, wheat, oats, barley or apples at ground level if left along fence lines or backs of yards bordering farmlands and fields.

California Quail

Winter Range: Southwest British Columbia.

Habitat: Underbrush, roadsides, forest edges.

Description: Plump, predominantly brown bird, short tails, small heads, black teardrop topknot on head. *Male* — White band on black throat, gray chest. *Female* — Paler.

California Quail are often seen walking single file down country roads, often the female leading the young.

During the winter months they will sometimes appear at feeding grounds in rural locations when the ground is covered with snow. Quail will eat berries, acorns, sunflower seeds, wheat, corn and millet. Food should be left in a sheltered ground area.

Thrushes

American Robin

Winter Range: Eastern United States as far north as lower Great Lakes, increasing in the north.

Habitat: Cities, towns, lawns, farmlands, wooded areas, cherry trees.

Description: 10". Rust-colored chest, dark gray wings, back, head, tail, lighter white on stomach area. Female —Paler coloring.

Once considered the first sign of spring, the Robin is increasing its winter range ever farther northwards. Robins often come to our gardens not so much for the use of feeding stations as for worms found in our lawns and cherries in our orchards. Robins that winter over in the more northerly limits of their range may take food from feeders in extremely bad weather but are otherwise very independent.

Varied Thrush

Winter Range: Western and northeastern Canada, northern states, casual from west.

Habitat: Wooded areas, lawns, shrubs, wood edges.

Description: Similar coloring as Robin — chest a lighter yellow-orange with a black band. A light tan eyebrow may also be apparent.

Varied Thrush

This bird is often called the "winter Robin." The Varied Thrush is rarely seen at feeders in mild weather, but as soon as the ground is covered in white it comes to more populated areas in search of food. More and more of these birds are being recorded at feeding stations in the east. Varied Thrushes will eat raisins, currants, berries and apples.

Titmice

Black-capped Chickadee

Winter Range: Southern half of Canada, northern half of United States east of Rockies.

Habitat: Deciduous and coniferous forests, shrubs, underbrush, gardens.

Description: 5". Small-bodied, proportionately longer tail, black cap and bib, white cheeks, gray back, wings, tail.

Black-capped Chickadee

Chickadees are very tame, friendly birds that will easily come to your hand for sunflower seeds. Their "dee dee" notes often seem to be words of thanks. Taking one sunflower seed at a time, they will return repeatedly for their favorite food. They are selective and will take the best seeds first. If chickadees are sorting for long periods it may mean the seeds you have provided are of poor quality. Suet will also appeal to chickadees. Small feeders, hanging suet logs and peanuts allow chickadees variety for their acrobatics.

Chestnut-backed Chickadee

Winter Range: Western Canada, northwestern states west of Rockies.

Habitat: Mixed forests of mountain and coastal regions.

Description: Similar to Black-capped only more brown in color on back and body. This bird is the friendly west coast version of the Black-capped Chickadee.

Tufted Titmouse

Winter Range: Southern tip of Canada, Lake Erie, eastern half of United States.

Habitat: Wooded areas, groves, gardens.

Description: 5½". Small gray bird, small black bill, gray crest, light chest — warmer near tail, small white patch around eyes.

Tufted Titmouse

The Tufted Titmouse feeds in the same fashion as the chickadee, taking one sunflower seed at a time. Flying off to a branch, it hammers the shell apart to get at the inside kernel, then returns for another. They are just as capable as chickadees of hanging upside down if necessary to get at suet or anything difficult to reach.

The northern winter range of this bird is expanding owing to the increased popularity of winter feeding.

Water Fowl Mallard

Winter Range: Southern Great Lakes and most of United States.

Habitat: Marshes, ponds, lakes, rivers and farms.

Description: Iridescent green head, yellow bill, white neck ring, warm brown chest, black and white tail, gray to light gray wings and body, flash of iridescent blue on wings. Female — Mottled gray-brown body, same blue on wings.

Mallard

Mallards are common domestic ducks that live year-round in farm ponds. During the winter domestic ducks must be sheltered, watered and fed regularly, a daily task with wild Mallards. Regular daily feeding will keep them from flying south. A source of water nearly is a must if the pond or lake is prone to freezing. It is probably a good idea not to encourage these birds to stay over unless you have adequate facilities.

Mallards are heavy grain feeders and require grit in their diet to aid in digestion. Recommended feeds include wheat, corn, barley, oats, millet and scratch feeds.

American Black Duck

Winter Range: New Brunswick, Nova Scotia, southern Ontario, northeastern United States, Great Lakes, Minnesota to Florida. Northern limits receding.

Habitat: Marshes, lakes, rivers, ponds, Great Lakes.

Description: Male — Charcoal black body, lighter head, blue flash on wings, dirty yellow bill. Female — Lighter brown, mottled body, blue-purple flash on wings, lighter head. Both have white patches on underside of wings, visible in flight.

American Black Duck

The diet of the American Black Duck is similar to the Mallard. Both prefer to feed in the water where they hold themselves upside down, heads under water, leaving their tails and bodies bobbing on the surface.

To feed these ducks, offer various grains in shallow water where they can reach the bottom with their bills.

Canada Goose

Winter Range: Eastern seaboard, Great Lakes, south central United States, Mexico.

Habitat: Lakes, shores, grain fields, ponds.

Description: 40". Long black neck and head, white band under chin. Light gray chest, darker gray-brown wings, white and black tail feathers.

Canada Goose

Canada Geese will consume feed brought to them in areas where they are regularly fed, such as grain mills and public parks bordering lakes. The majority of these birds migrate south of the Great Lakes in the fall as far as Mexico.

Regular feeding in sanctuaries, farm ponds and urban parks have helped large numbers to winter over in the southern points of Ontario and the Great Lakes.

They will eat wheat, corn, barley, oats.

Waxwings   Cedar Waxwing

Winter Range: Travels extensively through most areas south of the 49⁰ parallel, Great Lakes to Panama.

Habitat: Coniferous forests, berry-producing trees and shrubs.

Description: Smooth, gray bodies and wings, gray slick crest with black bill and eye slash, red on tips of wings, yellow band on tail end.

Cedar Waxwing

Waxwings will most likely be attracted to your yard by berry-producing shrubs rather than by food at your feeders. Most waxwings will not stay long at feeding grounds but will eat raisins, currants or apples when winter conditions are severe.

Wood-peckers

Downy Woodpecker

Winter Range: Alaska, Canada to southern United States, Newfoundland to Florida.

Habitat: Wooded areas, treed gardens, wood lots.

Description: 6"-7". White underside and back, black wings with white flecks, black and white head and tail, well-defined markings. Male — Red patch on back of head.

Downy Woodpecker

Downy Woodpeckers are a common sight in most wooded areas, where they feed higher up on the tree trunks. Insects and insect larvae are its natural foods, easily substituted for at our feeders with suet and suet-seed mixes. Downies are energetic woodpeckers that can become quite tame, sometimes taking food from the hand. Suet logs and suet smeared on tree bark will accommodate Downies. They will also eat sunflower seeds and corn meal.

Hairy Woodpecker

Winter Range: Same as Downy Woodpecker.

Habitat: Wooded areas, groves, wood lots, treed garden areas.

Description: 9". Almost identical markings as Downy but with larger and more developed bill.

The Hairy Woodpecker is a little more timid than the Downy, but nevertheless it is a regular visitor at suet feeders and feeders bearing sunflower seeds and corn. The Hairy Woodpecker can make a loud, hammering noise when pursuing insects in the bark of infested trees. They pause periodically in their industrious pounding, cocking their heads to see more accurately what they are doing.

FEEDING WILD BIRDS IN WINTER

Common Flicker
(Yellow-shafted, Red-shafted)

Winter Range: Yellow-shafted — Southern parts of Great Lakes, eastern half of United States; Red-shafted — West coast regions of North America.

Habitat: Woodlots, mixed vegetation farms, gardens, orchards.

Description: Yellow-shafted — The yellow undersides of this bird are revealed in flight. Chest is speckled, end of tail feathers is black, mottled black and brown wings, red spot on back of head, upper chest has definite black band. Well-developed bill. Male has black "moustache" patch. Red-shafted — Same as Yellow-shafted but yellow underside and male's black "moustache" replaced by red. Also, no red spot on backs of head.

The Red-shafted Flicker is the western version of the Common Flicker, while the Yellow-shafted tends to occur mainly in the east. They are a common sight in areas of dead trees. Their long bills allow them to probe the ground in search of ants and other insects. In the winter flickers will come to feeders bearing suet, but generally they are rare guests.

Pileated Woodpecker

Winter Range: James Bay to Florida, eastern half of North America, west coast regions.

Habitat: Coniferous and deciduous forests.

Description: 19". Large black woodpecker, white on underside of wings, white line from bill down neck to underside of wing, brilliant red crest.

Pileated Woodpecker

Pileated Woodpeckers will sometimes come to feeders, but they are very wary of man. In forest regions of the west coast they are even less likely to appear at feeders, the winter conditions being more moderate and the food supply greater. If they appear at all, they are more at home on tree trunks where suet can be provided for them.

Wrens

Winter Wren

Winter Range: Southeastern states as far north as lower Great Lakes and Cape Cod.

Habitat: Wooded areas, underbrush, wood piles.

Description: 4". A small, plump bird with tiny, upturned tail, warm brown color, lighter on throat and chest.

Winter Wren

The Winter Wren feeds close to the ground in areas of thick underbrush and shrubbery. They are rarely seen at feeders, for they are extremely timid birds. They prefer to stay out of sight in woodpiles and stacks of dead branches. The only wren that inhabited my woodpile was eaten by a cat.

City Birds

It is easy enough to overlook some of the more familiar birds of our cities and towns. As a generally accepted, or at least tolerated, part of the urban landscape they can become invisible through overfamiliarity.

This group of adaptable birds have managed to survive in spite of the unnatural elements of our ever-changing cities. Rather than flee the smells, noise and chaos, these birds have stayed with us, taking advantage of our charity and waste to alleviate their environmental hardships.

Pigeons (Feral and Domestic)

Year-round Range: Worldwide domestication, occurs in all populated areas of North America.

Habitat: Buildings, bridges, farms, parks, cities, towns.

Description: 13." Original coloring, cool gray with iridescent colors on neck area. Wings have black bands on top, fan-shaped tail. Cross-breeding has brought about various colorings — browns, white, black and multi-colored.

Pigeon (Feral)

City squares, bus terminals and parks are favorite feeding grounds for pigeons. Groups of people at leisure waiting for the next train or having lunch in a park will usually be the audience for a parade of these avian bread-mongers.

Despite the fact that cities offer these birds widespread and regular food, they also subject them to many perils. The increasingly high buildings have created gusty wind tunnels. When there is no wind, buildings act as barriers holding traffic exhaust in high concentrations. Rooftops—pigeons' favorite roosts—are a maze of guy wires and antennaes.

Once while working on the third floor of a factory I noticed a pigeon flapping its wings as it slowly slid down the roof of an adjacent building. A closer look revealed a leg missing. After reaching the gutter the bird broke into flight, circling the building several times before attempting another landing. Again it slid down the slate roof on its belly, using its wings to slow itself down. When reaching the gutter this time it was able to stop and support itself on its single leg.

Whether this bird survived its amputation and managed to compete with the other pigeons for food, I don't know. I only wondered if the tangle of wires on that roof had been the cause of this bird's crippling. How many others suffer the same fate flying about the rooftops of cities in the fog and snow?

Bread seems to be the single most important dietary item for pigeons. There is a never-ending supply offered to them daily in our city parks and squares. In North America discarded food comes in many forms: french fries, hot dogs, hamburger buns, ice cream cones and lunch bag contents are a few of the items left behind for them.

Regular flocks hang about fast food premises where they are able to pick up a variety of titillating foods. The quantity of discarded food around these outlets is astonishing. Because these places are usually open long hours, I am sure these birds must have a breakfast, lunch and dinner menu.

Pigeons do not often visit feeding stations, but when they do, they will eat more nutritious foods such as corn, wheat, millet and rice.

House Sparrow

Year-round Range: Worldwide, almost all of North America.

Habitat: Cities, farms, fields, gardens, barns.

Description: 6″. Chestnut-brown wings and tail, lighter chest. Male — Black throat patch with white patch on side of neck. Female — Paler.

Eating right alongside the pigeons will often be that nervous little bird the ubiquitous House Sparrow. Introduced in North America (Brooklyn) in 1850, it has steadily increased in population.

These birds manage to get along quite well with other city birds, for they will pick up most of the tiny morsels overlooked by others.

During the winter months they dart about, landing on clear patches of pavement where the salt has melted the snow away, in search of anything edible. At feeders they will eat most foods.

Feed mills, grain elevators, farmyards and unloading facilities attract large flocks of House Sparrows, where they feast on the great quantities of spilled grain. At certain times of the year they migrate along with masses of people to the many fairs and exhibitions where rows of concession stands offer a variety of fine found foods.

The next time you take a bite of anything outside, look down at the ground and you will probably see the crumbs of a House Sparrow's lunch.

Herring Gull

Year-round Range: Northern parts of North America, Great Lakes, east and west coasts.

Habitat: Shores of lakes, rivers, oceans, bays, piers, docks, pilings, farmlands, garbage dumps.

Description: 25″. Gray wings with black tips, white body, tail and head, yellow bill wth red spot, flesh-colored legs.

The Herring Gull, commonly known as the "seagull," has a variety of haunts. They can be seen trailing fishing boats and ships, waiting for kitchen scraps and free handouts.

Not only are they found along ocean coasts, bays, beaches, rivers and lakes, but they will also travel inland.

Large, screaming flocks follow farm tractors in the course of spring or fall plowing. The freshly overturned soil exposes many worms and grubs for them to pounce on. Never landing for long, they usually keep pace with the plow, grabbing newly exposed worms before they have a chance to disappear back into the dark, wet soil.

Garbage dumps are another favorite haunt. Unlike crows and blackbirds they are not frightened away by machinery. Trucks and bulldozers turning over fresh fare only temporarily interrupt their scavenging. If the dump is no longer in use, or is not being continuously added to, the gulls will move off, leaving the grounds for crows and other scavengers. Gulls will not attend feeding stations but can be fed in parks, waterfront areas and harbours.

Starling (European)

Winter Range: Southern Canada and United States.

Habitat: Cities, farms, generally feeding at ground level.

Description: Iridescent black with white speckling in winter, underside brownish-black, yellow bill, stubby tail.

Starling

The Starling is probably the most familiar bird in North America. It was introduced to this continent in New York's Central Park where sixty birds were released in 1890, another forty in 1891. Needless to say, it has been very successful. Giant populations now inhabit most of North America. The Starling's migration in the fall is only partial. Many birds winter over, congregating in populated areas to feed on park leftovers, bread and garbage. Basically ground-feeding birds, Starlings can be useful to the gardener, for their diet includes grass root destroying grubs.

The Starling's winter coloring is almost black with pronounced light speckling over much of the body. In the spring and fall the speckles are less obvious and there is more iridescence to the plumage.

If all attempts to attract other birds to your feeding grounds fail, you can always count on the appearance of a few Starlings. However, if you are overly successful, the noise these birds can create while feeding may cause your neighbors to become rather hostile.

Starlings eat much the same foods we do. Almost anything you give them will be relished.

3 Food

The little grain of wheat, tritucum, is the noblest food of man. The lesser grains of other grasses are the food of passerine birds at present. Their diet is like man's.

H. THOREAU, WALDEN

Dried sunflower

The simplest bird feeding program involves little more than throwing some stale bread crumbs onto the snow. But once this casual regimen begins attracting some interesting avian visitors, you may well decide to attempt something more ambitious.

At this point you might introduce a bag of bird mix available at garden centres, hardware stores, some supermarkets and pet stores. These mixes usually contain sunflower seeds, crushed corn, wheat, millet, buckwheat and some lesser grains. Proportions in these mixes vary from brand, but they will give you an idea of what the birds in your area prefer. If most of the smaller grain is left over, you will obviously have to increase the proportions of crushed corn and sunflower seeds. Along with the wild bird mix you should also try some of the other items listed in this chapter.

The most widely accepted and popular foods are sunflower seeds, crushed corn, and suet. Make an effort to try these three. In doing so you will be appealing to the tastes of a wide variety of birds. These favorite foods are available in bulk at a fraction of the cost of prepackaged mixes. For suet feeding you may need the instructions for easy-to-build suet feeders found in chapter 4.

Having established which items you will need daily, you should consider bulk purchasing, as it is time-saving and economical. Sunflower seeds, whole kernel or crushed corn, peanut hearts, millet, oats, wheat, buckwheat, barley and rapeseed are available in large quantities from feed mills (that cater to farms) and some garden centres.

Suet (stringy white masses of beef fat) is available by the pound from your butcher. Keep it refrigerated or frozen. A few pounds will last a month or more depending on how well you discourage the squirrels.

Grain and seed are best stored in a dry, cool place. Keep separately or mixed to your proportions in plastic garbage bags secured with twist ties. To keep mice out and bags intact it may be necessary to put the bags in a covered or metal garbage can. Keep a tin can inside for serving out daily amounts.

GRAINS AND SEEDS

Sunflower Seeds

This is the best all-purpose seed. It is nutritious (high in protein, fats and carbohydrates), economical and a choice food for almost all winter birds. If you have the garden space and a sunny, protected area (against a fence or wall), sunflowers are easily cultivated. Grow the commercial variety rather than the ornamental one as the seeds are larger and more palatable. The whole flower head may be offered once it has been cut off and sun-dried. Keep a large stock of these seeds available in February and March when the greedy flocks of Evening Grosbeaks strike your feeders. Use in hopper-type feeders, on feeding tables, window shelves, or scatter these dark seeds on a packed snow surface where they can easily be seen.

You can expect almost all birds to take sunflower seeds at some time, but they are the favorite seeds of: chickadees (Boreal, Black-capped and Chestnut-backed), Cardinals, Rose-breasted Grosbeaks, Steller's Jays, Slate-colored Juncos, Mourning Doves, all sparrows, Purple Finches, Pine Siskins, Grackles, all nuthatches, Tufted Titmice.

Corn

Corn is eaten by almost all of the winter birds. Use whole, crushed and milled (corn meal) for maximum appeal. Corn left standing in your garden through the winter will offer a natural source for some birds skillful enough to penetrate the leafy husks. Stalks of corn tied up in sheaf fashion and stacked close to treelined fields and orchards can offer shelter and food for Bobwhites, Ruffed Grouse and Ring-necked Pheasants. Some of the corn should, however, be re-

Dried corn: whole cob, kernels, crushed, cornmeal.

moved from the stalks and left on the ground underneath. You can count on buying corn, like sunflower seeds, in large quantities. Corn works well in hopper-type feeders, on feeding tables or ground scattered. It is also excellent used in scratch feed (discussed later in this chapter).

Corn is the favorite of these birds: Cardinals, Cowbirds, Crows, doves (Rock, Mourning, Band-tailed), Canada Geese, Grackles, Red-breasted Grosbeaks, Slate-colored Juncos, Ducks, Ruffed Grouse, Ring-necked Pheasants, Ravens, sparrows, Rufous-sided Towhees, Hairy Woodpeckers, flickers, Evening Grosbeaks.

Wheat

Wheat seed whole or cracked has a great appeal for a wide variety of birds. If you are fortunate enough to have a pond on your property, you might like to start regular feeding of ducks and geese in the summer months, encouraging them to stay over the winter. Wheat and similar grains are their favorite food. Harvested wheat fields sometimes have patches of knocked down stalks or small areas the combines have missed. Collect and tie up fistfuls of these stalks. Propped in the snow with the heads exposed they will provide food for the birds and entertainment for you. At the back of your property there may be a tree-lined fence where you can tie bunches of wheat together for the pheasants to find.

Wheat is the choice food of blackbirds (Red-winged), Snow Buntings, Cardinals, Cowbirds, American Crows, Mourning Doves, Pigeons, Mallards, Black Ducks, Canada Geese, Grackles, Rose-breasted Grosbeaks, jays (Blue, Canada, Steller's), Slate-colored Juncos, Ring-necked Pheasants, most sparrows, Rufous-sided Towhees and Starlings.

Millet

There are quite a few different types of millet, but they all have the same nutritional and taste appeal. Millet seed, because of its small size, is ideal for including in suet recipes (cakes). Scatter millet on the ground or on feeding tables so that it is more accessible to the ground-feeding birds. It is a favorite of the Cardinal, Mourning Dove, pigeon (Rock Dove), Purple Finch, Gold Finch, Canada Goose, Slate-colored Junco, Mallard, Redpoll and most sparrows.

Hemp Seed

Because hemp is also the plant that produces marijuana, government regulations have made it necessary to blanch and sterilize the seeds before being taken to the market. Sterilization makes the seeds less desirable for birds. It is still

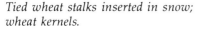

Tied wheat stalks inserted in snow; wheat kernels.

73   FOOD

one of the seeds found in wild bird mixes. This seed should be used in a similar manner as millet. Birds that eat millet will generally take hemp seed as a replacement.

Rice

Although not as popular as wheat, rice can be used as a substitute. Both cooked and uncooked rice are acceptable. Obviously, brown rice will be more nutritious than the processed, adulterated versions. However, the great nutritional value of carbohydrates can be derived from all rice types.

Birds that will eat rice include the Cardinal, Red-winged Blackbird, Rock Dove, most ducks and geese, Slate-colored Junco, most sparrows and the Mourning Dove.

Oats

Used in seed form, crushed, rolled or in the form of solidified porridge, oats will appeal to most blackbirds, Cardinals, Rufous-sided Towhees, most sparrows, Ring-necked Pheasants, Slate-colored Juncos, Grackles, grosbeaks and Rock Doves.

Cultivated Sorghum

Sorghum seeds are favorite foods of Cardinals, Mourning Doves, Grackles, Blue Jays, Slate-colored Juncos and most sparrows.

Rapeseed

Rape is a plant belonging to the mustard family and grown extensively in the prairie regions. The seed is a favorite of the Mourning Dove, Gold Finch, Purple Finch, Slate-colored Junco and the redpoll.

Buckwheat

Usually found in prepared wild bird mixes, it can also be purchased from feed mills. Having bought a suitable quantity of these small, pyramid-shaped hard seeds, you will be able to add it to your own homemade mixes in a proportion suitable to the demand.

Buckwheat (common variety) is a favorite food of Cardinals, American Crows, Ruffed Grouse, Ring-necked Pheasants, Mourning Doves and sparrows.

SCRATCH FEED

Scratch feed is generally used commercially for feeding chickens. However, it is a good idea to provide small quantities of it for birds in your garden. The digestive system of birds requires the ingestion of small quantities of dirt to aid in the digestive process. Fine sand added in small quantities to smaller seeds such as millet, sorghum, rapeseed, wheat or crushed corn can provide a good scratch feed. Other essentials for birds such as salt and calcium (eggshell) may also be added. Offer scratch feeds along with other mixes or scatter occasionally on the ground.

SUET

Suet seems to fill the needs of all insect-eating birds. The fat is a high source of energy and heat necessary for birds in the winter. Cut off the loose, stringy pieces and save for melting down. Take the larger, whole pieces (about the size of a small fist) and wrap them entirely in plastic mesh bags, tied at one end (onion bags are excellent for this). Bags should be securely tied with string or twine to branches or suet feeders.

Melt down the stringy leftovers in a pot, pour into small containers and leave to set. Plastic or paper cups are more suitable than metal ones, as there is no risk to the birds and they can be discarded after use. Suet served plain in this fashion is fine, or you can add any variety of nuts, seeds, currants, raisins, peanut butter, peanut hearts or corn. It is a great medium for holding together all your birds' favorite recipes. A few words of caution: 1) Do not use wire mesh, metal screening or wire to secure suet; 2) Tie down securely with twine so larger birds and squirrels won't disappear with the whole piece; 3) Remove all old stringy suet from feeders in warm weather to prevent it from turning rancid; 4) keep out of reach of dogs.

Save the grease and drippings from bacon and oven-cooked meats for use in the same manner as suet. Because the consistency of these fats is generally softer than suet, it is advisable to use them in the recipe mixes mentioned above. Almost all birds will eat suet in one form or another.

BREAD AND PROCESSED FOODS

Bread is a staple item not only of our diet but of city-dwelling birds' too. It is very useful for controlling birds at your feeding station. Start putting out bread at the beginning of the winter season, and as soon as the offerings have brought in flocks of Starlings and House Sparrows, other species are sure to follow their example. When your bird population starts to get out of hand and overcrowding is becoming a problem, move the bread further away from feeders and reduce the daily quantities. If the Starling and House Sparrow population is still too large, try skipping a day or so. The practice of feeding bread to city-dwelling birds is worldwide. Great quantities are fed to pigeons (Rock Doves), Starlings and House Sparrows in city parks. Ducks, geese and seagulls are also used to the taste of bread and compete with each other for the larger pieces. Scatter the bread widely in an area where there are numerous birds waiting for your charity. Remember that whole grain bread has more nutritional value for birds.

Crackers, muffins, pastry crust, whole wheat and other breakfast cereals, popcorn, biscuits and hard dog meal may be offered, but you run the risk of attracting dogs, more

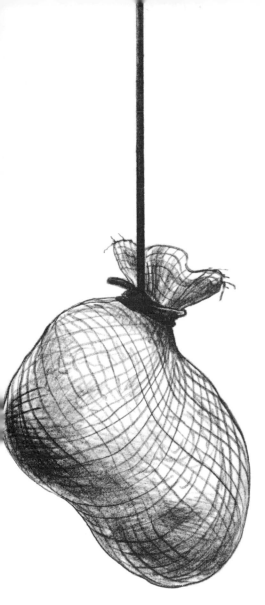

Suet tied in plastic mesh onion bag.

Melted suet and seeds poured into disposable container.

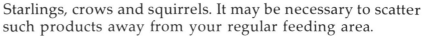

Small pieces are peanut hearts.

Starlings, crows and squirrels. It may be necessary to scatter such products away from your regular feeding area.

NUTS

All nuts are nutritious as they contain protein, carbohydrates, fats and vitamins. They are too expensive to offer birds on a regular bulk basis, but small quantities added periodically may entice some birds to your feeders that would not otherwise come. Collecting indigenous nuts such as acorns, chestnuts, beech nuts and walnuts before the squirrels hide them all will add variety to your feeding program and help keep down costs.

Peanuts

Unshelled peanuts are rather difficult for smaller birds to penetrate. However, you might enjoy the antics of some birds trying to get at the nutmeats inside. So that larger birds and squirrels don't walk off with the whole lot, tie a group of larger peanuts together with thick nylon or linen thread and hang from your roof eve or a tree branch.

One cheap way of purchasing peanuts for feed purposes is in the form of peanut hearts, the small knuckle that falls out when a single nutmeat separates in half. These small pieces are the by-products of the peanut industry. Peanut hearts are available at some feed mills. Peanut butter, although costly, can be added in small quantities to suet cakes, or spread on the bark of trees or dangling pine cones for birds to peck at. Making these kinds of treats for the birds is something children would enjoy. Occasional use of salted peanuts is fine. Salt is one of the items some birds develop a craving for

and eat intentionally. Peanuts are a favorite food of most blackbirds, Cardinals, Catbirds, chickadees (all), crows, pigeons, Purple Finches, Robins, Tufted Titmice, wrens, most sparrows, Slate-colored Juncos, most nuthatches and some woodpeckers.

Fancy Nutmeats

Fancy nutmeats such as walnuts, pecans, hazelnuts, cashews and almonds should be given only as a special treat, otherwise you may find your feeding grounds overrun with squirrels. Because squirrels covet these nuts so much, it is a good idea to feed them to the squirrels intentionally, unshelled and away from the birds. They work well as a temporary distraction.

Coconut

Coconut appeals to some birds such as chickadees. Use the fresh pieces out of a shell.

FRUIT

Apples and Pears

Certain varieties of apples and pears lend themselves better to bird-feeding than to human consumption. Orchards that have been neglected and wild trees produce smaller, scabby varieties. It is a good idea to collect baskets of these apples and pears and store them in a cold place for the birds. As long as they keep well they can be used as feed. Cut in half to expose the seeds inside. Crabapples have the same appeal.

Most apples and pears are well received by Blue Jays,

crows, Grackles, Ruffed Grouse, Starlings, waxwings, Ring-necked Pheasants and Hairy Woodpeckers.

Raisins and Currants

If there are bluebirds in your area, there is a good chance they may be enticed to your feeder by a supply of raisins and currants.

VEGETABLE AND VEGETABLE SEEDS

Most birds are not too interested in vegetables either raw or cooked. However, save the seeds from your pumpkins, squashes, canteloupes and watermelons. Wash them off and dry them. Birds such as Cardinals, chickadees, Blue Jays and nuthatches will eat them.

A CHECKLIST OF FAVORITE FOODS

Foods	Birds Attracted
Apricots	Crows
Blackberries, summer and fall Raspberries	Bluebirds, Bobwhites, Cardinals, Catbird, Mockingbirds, orioles, Grackles, Blue Jays, juncos, Starlings.
Cherries — pincherries and chokecherries	Bluebirds, grosbeaks, Ruffed Grouse, Robins, flickers
Cherries, sweet Cover your cherry trees with mesh to keep birds off if you want to harvest — don't use thread or wire.	Bluebirds, Bobwhites, Cardinals, Catbirds, crows, flickers, grosbeaks, Ruffed Grouse, Blue Jays, kingbirds, Robins, woodpeckers, towhees, Grackles.
Cranberries	Robins, crows
Currants	Bluebirds, Robins, Brown Thrashers, Ruffed Grouse
Hawthorn berries, red Collect in fall for winter	Ruffed Grouse, Cedar Waxwings, Ring-necked Pheasants
Holly berries	Yellow-shafted Flickers, Robins, Bluebirds, Mockingbirds, Brown Thrashers
Peas — shelled fresh, or dried	Crows, Grackles, grosbeaks, Mallards, Ring-necked Pheasants

Peaches — dried	Catbirds, Purple Finches, Blue Jays, Mockingbirds, Robins, Brown Thrashers
Plums Prunes — dried	Catbirds, Blue Jays, Mockingbirds, Robins, Brown Thrashers, Grackles, flickers, Rufous-sided Towhees.
Strawberries	Catbird, crows, Robins, Starlings
Sugar water — provided in special feeders	Hummingbirds (summer only)
Meat, cheese, table scraps	Starlings, House Sparrows, sea-gulls, blackbirds, crows.
Berries	Blackbirds, Catbirds, Cardinals, crows, pigeons, flickers, Grackles, grosbeaks, most sparrows, Robins, Mockingbirds, jays, grouses, sparrows, Starlings, thrushes, thrasher, towhees, vireos, waxwings, woodpeckers.
Dry seeds	Blackbirds, buntings, Cardinals, cowbirds, crows, doves, ducks, finches, geese, Grackles, jays, juncos, Ring-necked Pheasants, redpolls, Pine Siskins, sparrows, thrashers, titmice, towhees.
Nuts	Cardinals, Catbirds, crossbills, crows, finches, Grackles, grosbeaks, jays, juncos, nuthatches, siskins, Starlings, thrashers, titmice, towhees, woodpeckers, wrens.

4

Feeders

Woodsheds can provide good shelter to feed birds such as juncos and wrens.

Each individual bird has it's own particular feeding behavior. This diversity in bird behavior demands a corresponding diversity in feeder design. Cardinals are more apt to use a feeder that has a perch, juncos prefer ground feeding and woodpeckers like vertical hanging feeders or something resembling a tree trunk.

If you wish to ground feed, there are a number of locations appropriate for scattering food. The lower branches of large, thick spruce, fir and hemlock may keep some of the snow from covering your feed. Hollow logs, wood piles, woodsheds or cleared pathways in the snow can offer some shelter and cover for ground-foraging birds. If feeding near or under evergreens, check to make sure that there is nothing close enough to conceal cats. Cedar hedges may provide good shelter, but they are usually thick enough to hide a waiting cat.

There are a number of things to consider before deciding what kind of feeder to buy or build. If you are buying, choose a simple design that's easy to clean and keep stocked up. Better feeders are usually made of rot resistant redwood or cedar. These woods weather well and turn a silvery gray color that blends in well with the landscape. Avoid buying metal feeders, which may have sharp edges, rust-prone areas and which may freeze up badly after a slight thaw. The eyes and tongues of birds can freeze to metal surfaces in extremely cold weather if they happen to make accidental contact.

Plastic feeders are available, but generally I have found them too flimsy and lightweight. They tend to break and blow in the wind, spilling most of the seed on the ground. However, there are some smaller plastic feeders that are quite useful.

All hopper-type feeders (feeders that only allow a certain amount of seed out at a time) should always be stationary. If they are hung up, they should be secured in some fashion to prevent excessive wind movement which can allow a needless flow of seed to escape. The best solution is to fix them securely on a post, metal pole (see illustration) or directly on the side of a tree (which has the possible disadvantage of providing squirrels with too easy an access).

If you build, don't weatherproof wood with preservatives. Almost all preservatives are poisonous. Feeders dry out quickly in the air and rot should not be much of a problem.

One last word of caution: it may be necessary to use some device to inhibit squirrels from rapidly emptying your feeders. (See illustrations and chapter 5: Problems and Solutions.)

GROUND TABLES OR PLATFORMS

A ground table is extremely simple to make and is effective for feeding ground-foraging and perching birds. It consists of a sheet of plywood or several boards nailed together which make up an area of approximately six square feet (2' x 3' is a good size). Attach the platform to legs to raise it about two feet off the ground (higher in areas of greater snowfall). A wooden lip around the perimeter (a nailed-on slat) will keep the feed from being blown or knocked off. The lip also serves as a grip for perching birds. This type of feeder should be placed in an open but sheltered area of your yard. If the table is placed just slightly off level, it will allow drainage in the event of rain or a quick thaw. Make a few holes at the lowest end. Easy access for you should be considered when positioning the table, as you will have to restock this type of feeder daily.

Smaller seed mixes (millet, crushed corn, buckwheat, wheat, etc.) and scratch feed works best with this feeder as they will appeal to the birds more than the squirrels. If the constant clearing of snow becomes a problem, a shallow pitched roof (shed or double-pitched) can always be added. However, leave the sides open to provide maximum entrance and exit routes.

Some small plastic hanging feeders appropriate for feeding smaller birds such as chickadees and titmice.

GROUND TABLE FEEDER

GROUND TABLE FEEDER

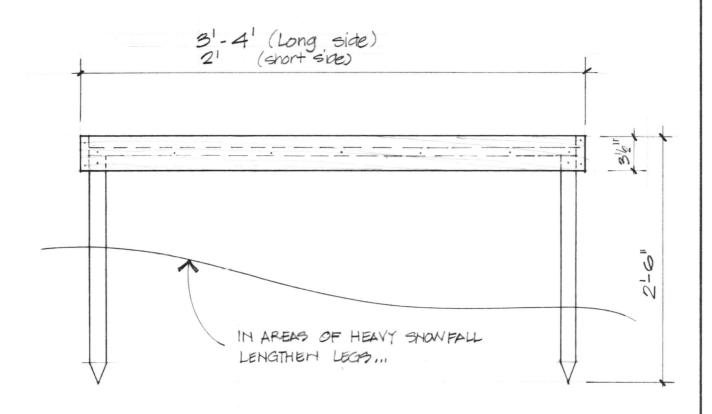

3' - 4' (Long side)
2' (short side)

3½"

2'-6"

IN AREAS OF HEAVY SNOWFALL
LENGTHEN LEGS...

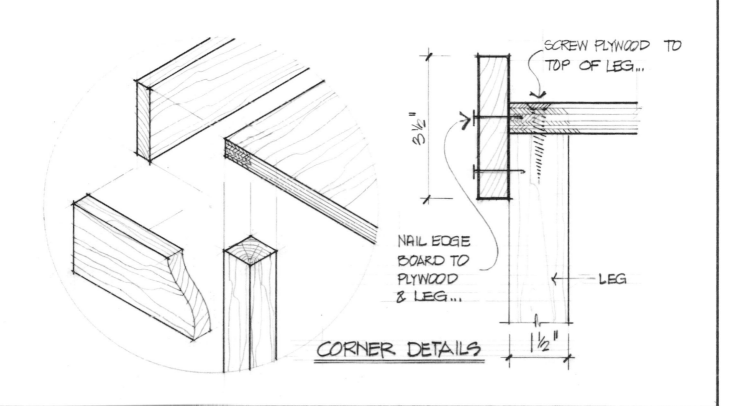

SCREW PLYWOOD TO
TOP OF LEG...

3½"

NAIL EDGE
BOARD TO
PLYWOOD
& LEG...

LEG

1½"

CORNER DETAILS

WINDOW SHELF FEEDERS

Window shelves are probably the best type of feeders for bird observation. Installation should take place sometime after you have been feeding birds from other feeders built away from your house. Birds that are regulars at your window shelf feeder will get used to glass surfaces and your movements on the other side more readily than the occasionals. These feeders are merely extensions of exterior windowsills. They should not project out from the wall further than one foot as drainage may become a problem. Again a lip around the outside is a good idea.

Some diagonal bracing may be necessary to provide extra support. If the window does not open, at least be sure you have a door nearby to allow easy access for restocking. This type of feeder may also be adapted to fit the top of an outside deck railing. Larger window shelf feeders (but not so large they become an obstruction) are useful for apartment dwellers and others who don't have convenient access to a backyard. If you are building the larger variety, be sure to provide drain holes.

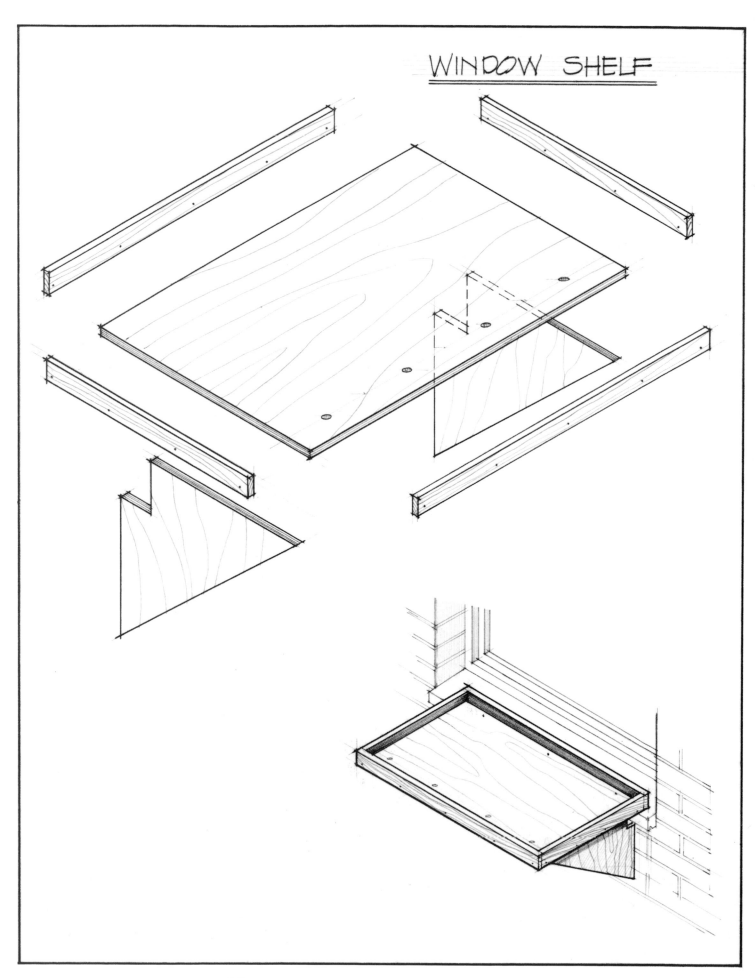

WINDOW SHELF

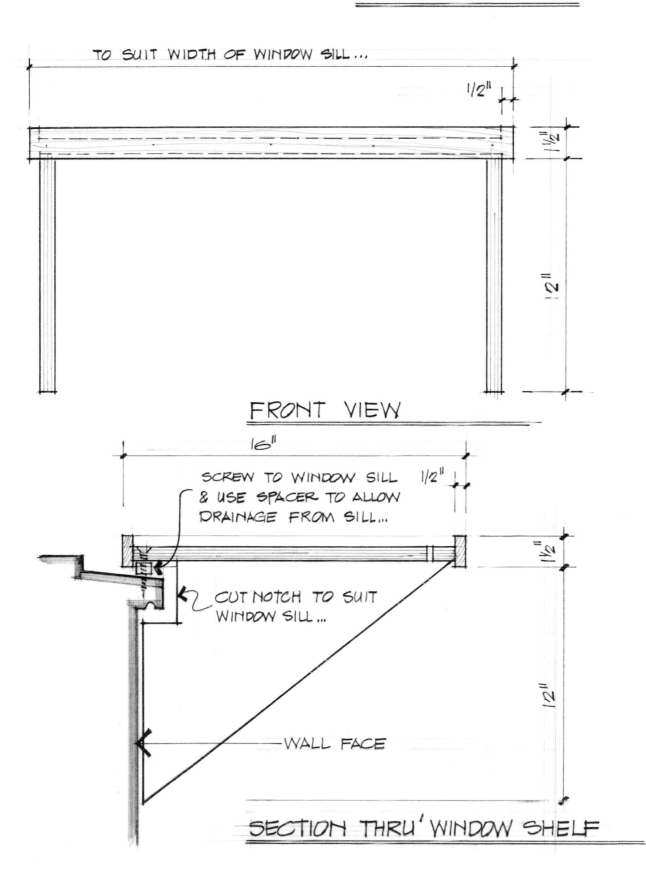

TO SUIT WIDTH OF WINDOW SILL...

1/2"

1/2"

12"

FRONT VIEW

16"

SCREW TO WINDOW SILL
& USE SPACER TO ALLOW
DRAINAGE FROM SILL...

1/2"

1/2"

CUT NOTCH TO SUIT
WINDOW SILL...

12"

WALL FACE

SECTION THRU' WINDOW SHELF

RAISED FEEDERS

Raised feeders have a number of advantages. If they are placed in an open sheltered area of your yard, they should be about head height (high enough to keep squirrels and cats out). They can be mounted on a wooden post (a fence post is fine) or metal pipe (see illustration for hardware). A square or rectangular base can be used, but surface feeding area should not exceed four square feet (24" x 18" is a good size). Any closed-in side should face the direction of prevailing winds to give additional shelter. A lip is necessary to contain food. This type of feeder is ideal for holding all types of food including suet cake mixes and suet bags. Provide an eye hook for securing suet bags.

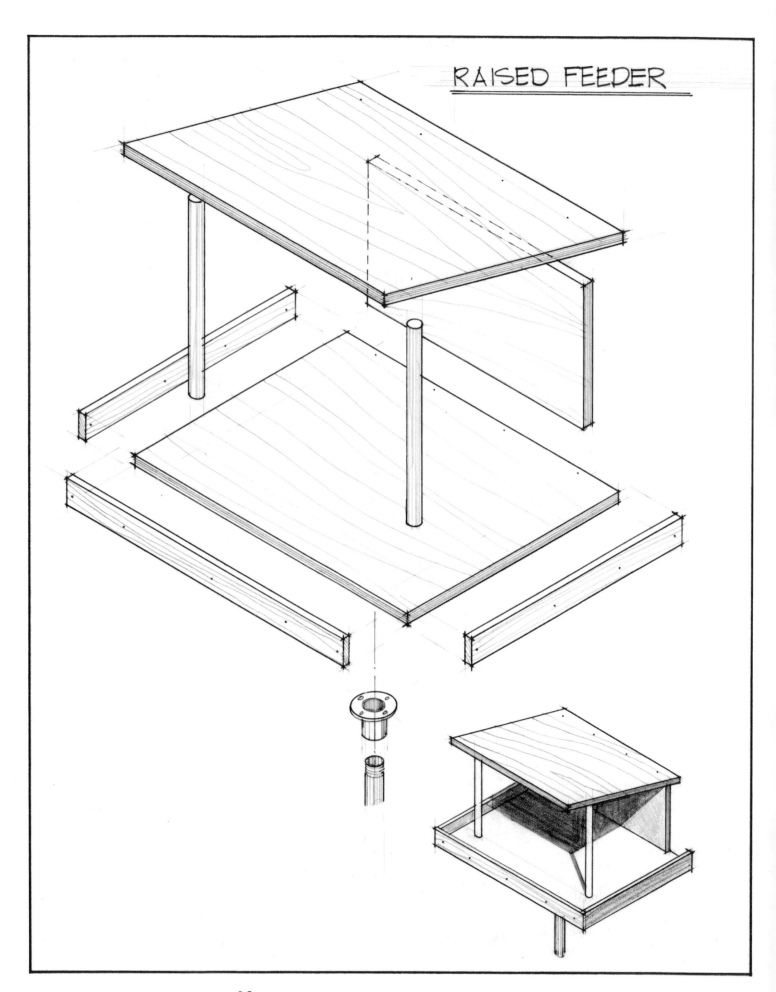

RAISED FEEDER

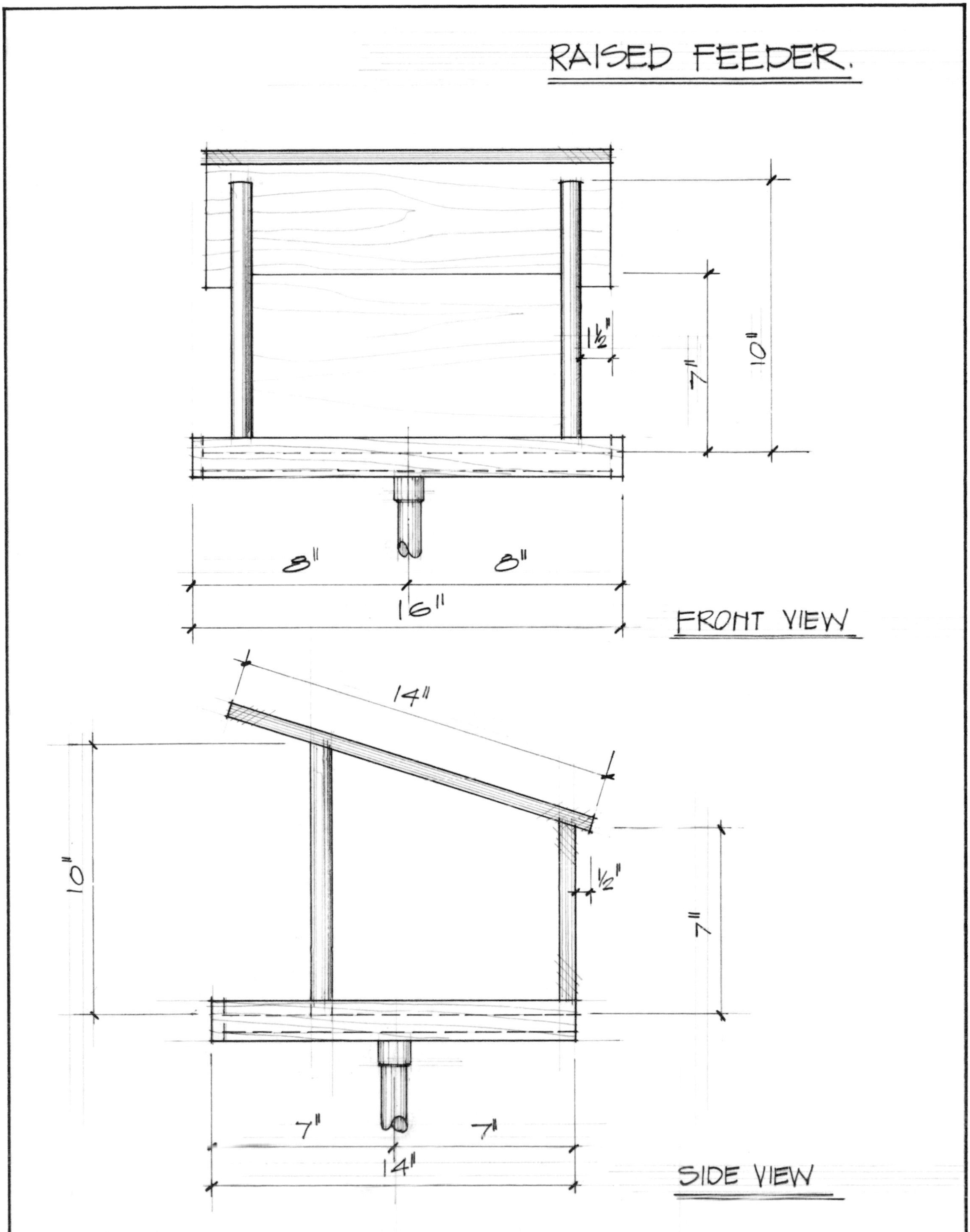

RAISED FEEDER.

FRONT VIEW

10"

7"

1½"

8"

8"

16"

SIDE VIEW

14"

10"

7"

½"

7"

7"

14"

HOPPER-TYPE FEEDERS

Hopper-type feeders are the most useful feeders for bulk distribution of seed and seed mixes. Depending on how many birds you have attending on a daily basis, it is possible for a large hopper feeder to slowly and automatically release its contents over a period of a week. This feature is most suitable for people who might be absent for a few days at a time. If you plan on winter holidays, a neighbor or friend may only have to refill your feeder once or twice during your absence. It is a good idea to mount the larger types of hopper feeders securely to a rigid post or pole. Avoid gimmicks in buying or constructing this type of feeder. They only cause problems. A good example is the popular weather vane version that has a tendency to seize up. Single-sided hopper types should be mounted directly to the side of a fence post or solid tree (see illustration).

When building these feeders avoid hinging the roof as a filling device. It weakens the structure and the joints will inevitably let in water. Instead drill a hole (1" diameter) large enough to insert a funnel for refilling. A slip cap or large cork can be used to close the hole. Use plexiglass, if possible, instead of glass for the sides that allow visible inspection of contents. It will make construction easier, stronger, safer. Plexiglass can be drilled and screwed, making it an integral part of the structure. Since these feeders carry more weight in feed than other types, take the time to build them properly. Make sure you leave the right size of gap for feed to escape (see specifications).

Commercial feeders come in so many shapes, sizes, colors and materials that I have only been able to illustrate a few. Most of the small hanging types are plastic and only allow room and feeding for one bird at a time. These types are more for fun and amusement than for functional feeding.

SUET FEEDERS

Suet feeding can be accomplished in a variety of ways. The simplest method is to tie up lumps of suet in small pieces of fishnet or plastic onion bags and lash them to the limb of a tree or fence post. The same may be tied to an eye hook installed inside a larger raised platform feeder.

A version of the single-sided hopper type can be constructed for suet feeding. Instead of installing glass you can provide some means of lashing in the suet.

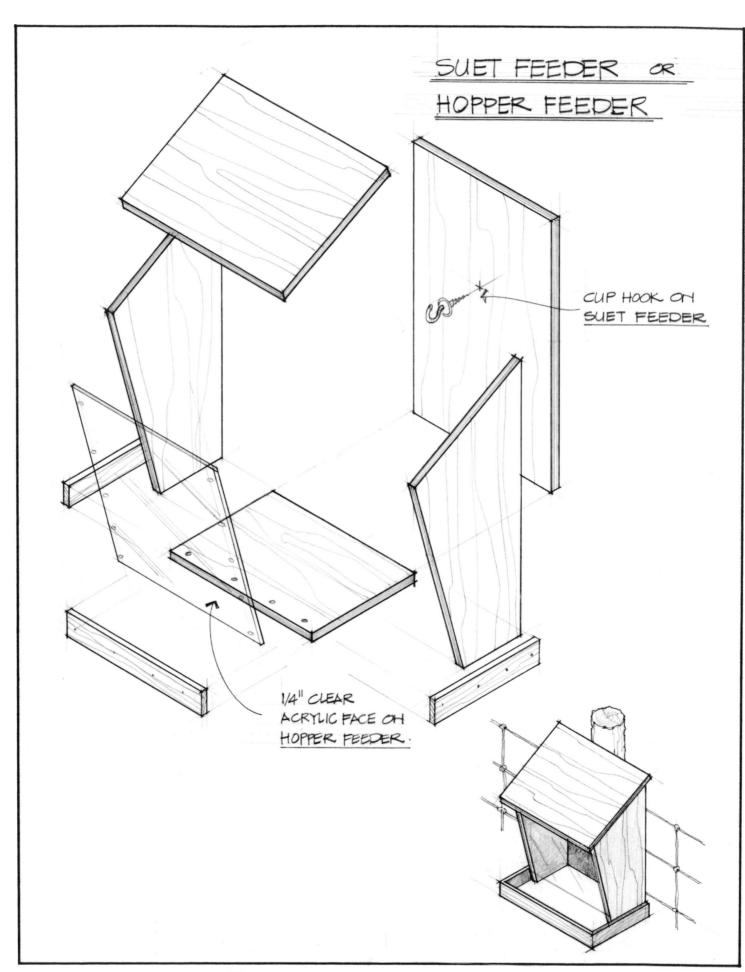

SUET FEEDER OR
HOPPER FEEDER

CUP HOOK ON
SUET FEEDER

1/4" CLEAR
ACRYLIC FACE ON
HOPPER FEEDER.

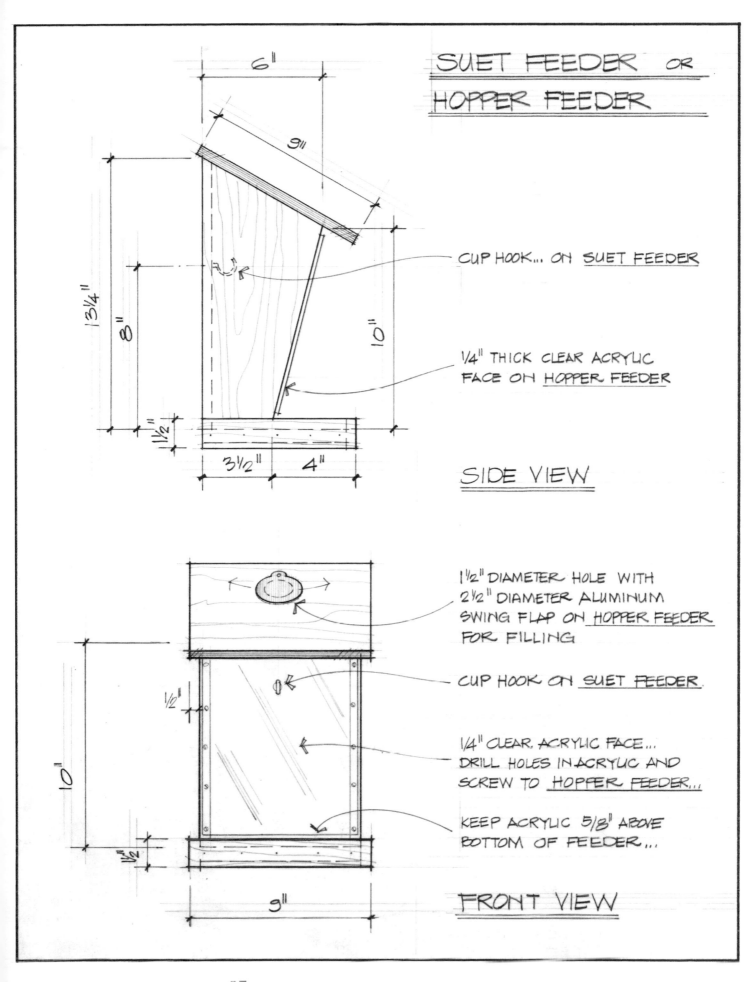

SUET FEEDER OR HOPPER FEEDER

6"

9"

CUP HOOK... ON SUET FEEDER

13¼"

8"

10"

¼" THICK CLEAR ACRYLIC FACE ON HOPPER FEEDER

1½"

3½"   4"

SIDE VIEW

1½" DIAMETER HOLE WITH 2½" DIAMETER ALUMINUM SWING FLAP ON HOPPER FEEDER FOR FILLING

CUP HOOK ON SUET FEEDER.

½"

¼" CLEAR ACRYLIC FACE... DRILL HOLES IN ACRYLIC AND SCREW TO HOPPER FEEDER...

10"

½"

KEEP ACRYLIC 5/8" ABOVE BOTTOM OF FEEDER...

9"

FRONT VIEW

DOUBLE HOPPER

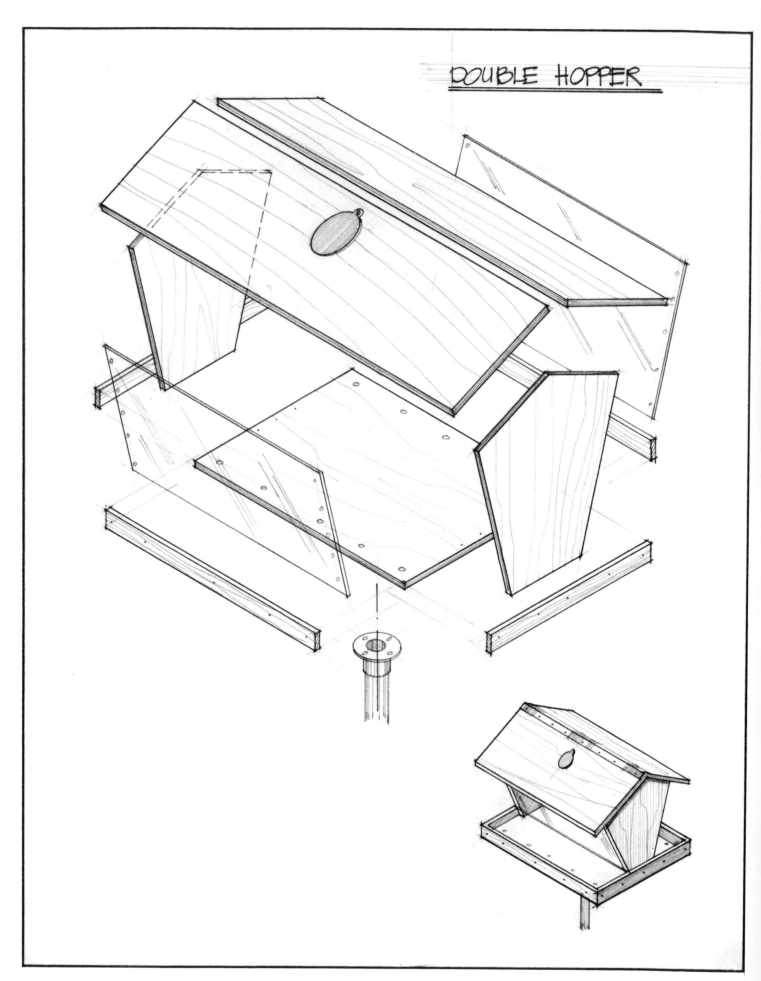

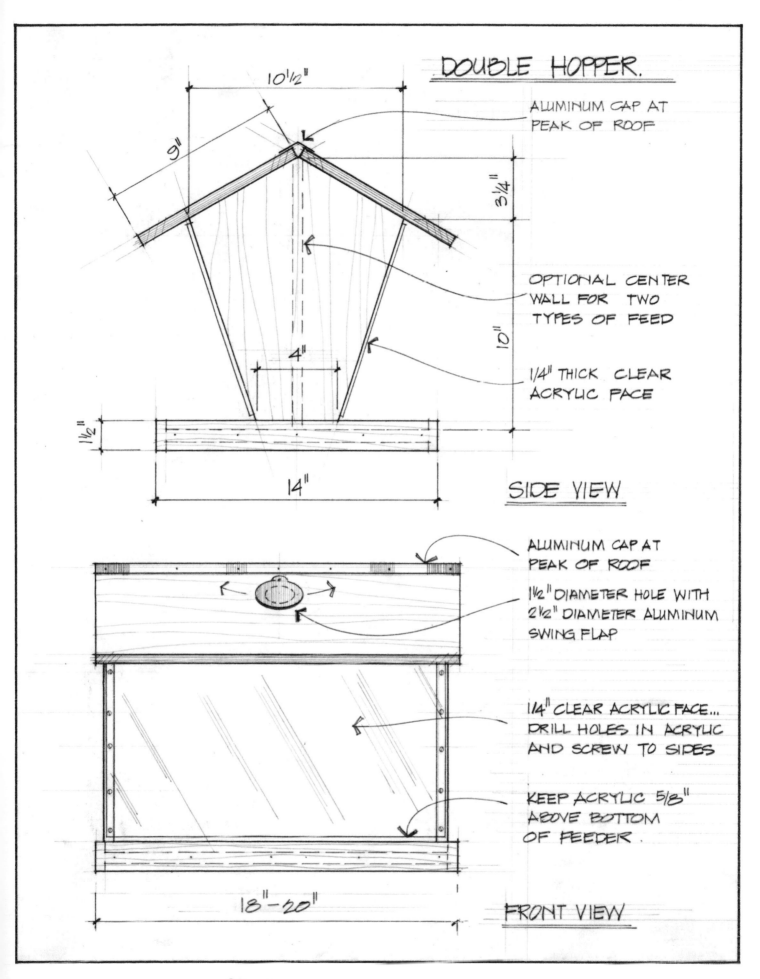

DOUBLE HOPPER.

10½"

9"

3¼"

ALUMINUM CAP AT
PEAK OF ROOF

OPTIONAL CENTER
WALL FOR TWO
TYPES OF FEED

10"

¼" THICK CLEAR
ACRYLIC FACE

4"

1½"

14"

SIDE VIEW

ALUMINUM CAP AT
PEAK OF ROOF

1½" DIAMETER HOLE WITH
2½" DIAMETER ALUMINUM
SWING FLAP

¼" CLEAR ACRYLIC FACE...
DRILL HOLES IN ACRYLIC
AND SCREW TO SIDES

KEEP ACRYLIC 5/8"
ABOVE BOTTOM
OF FEEDER.

18"-20"

FRONT VIEW

SUET LOG

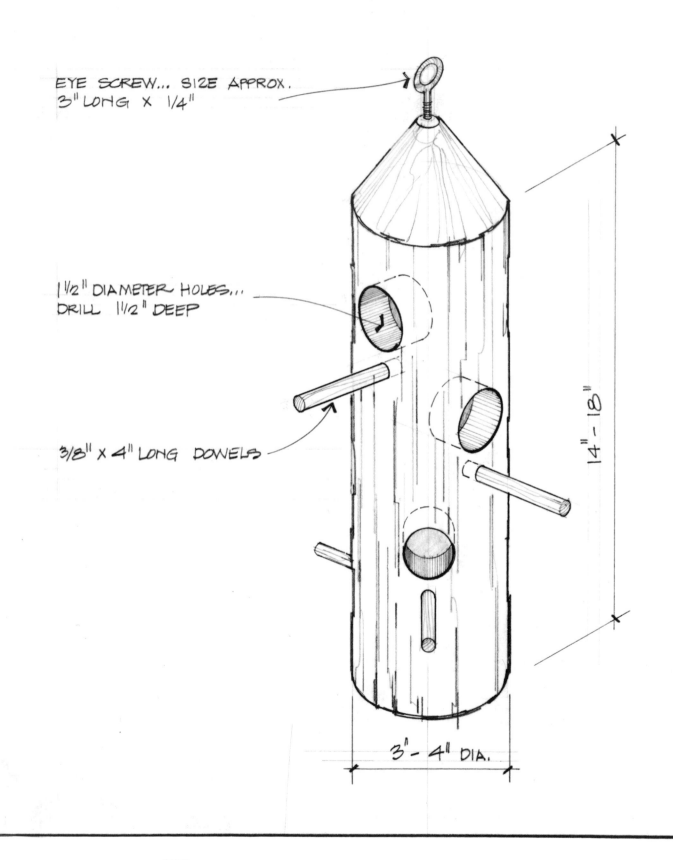

EYE SCREW... SIZE APPROX.
3" LONG × 1/4"

1 1/2" DIAMETER HOLES...
DRILL 1 1/2" DEEP

3/8" × 4" LONG DOWELS

14" - 18"

3" - 4" DIA.

SUET LOGS

A cedar, fir or hardwood log can make a great suet feeder. The log should be 3" - 4" in diameter and 14" - 18" long. Holes 1¼" - 1½" in diameter should be drilled 1½" deep. Melted suet and suet seed mixes can now be packed into the various holes. Hung by a large eye hook at one end, this vertical feeder is a favorite of woodpeckers. If you add some dowels (¼" diameter) for perches below the suet holes, other birds will be able to use it as well.

Rough bark left on the log will also allow birds of various kinds to get a grip while feeding. To avoid injury to birds make sure that the material you use to hang this feeder is quite visible — thick plastic-covered wire is ideal.

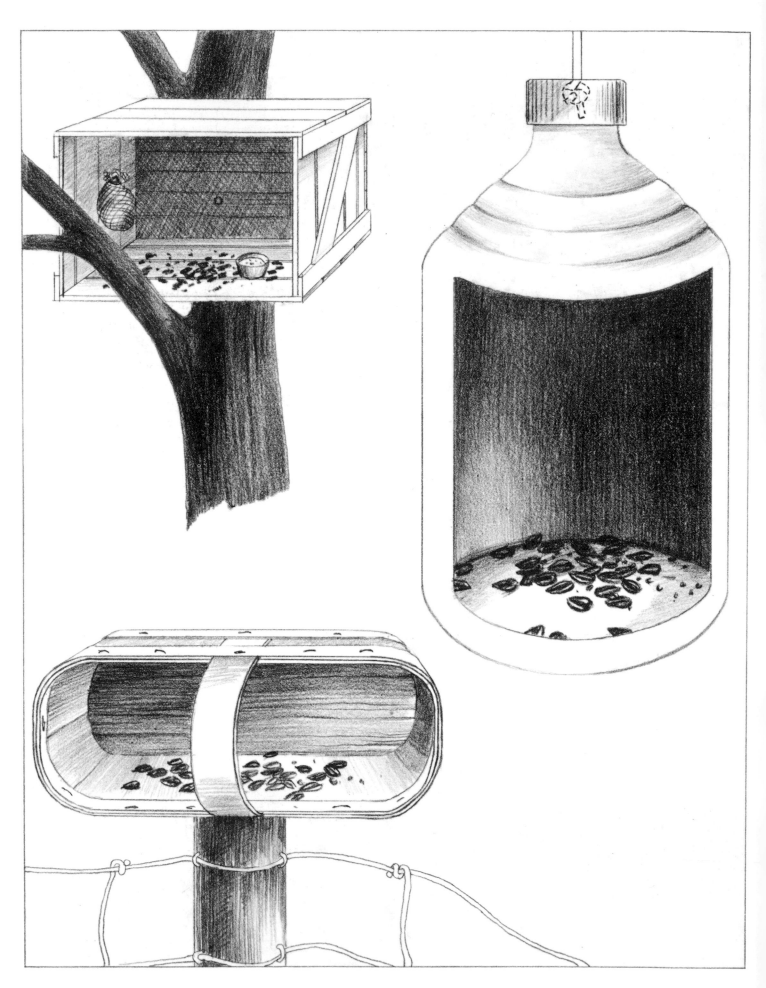

CHILDREN AND FEEDERS

Children, given some guidance, can enjoy themselves immensely making various kinds of feeders and bird recipes. Revised apple crates or grape crates make good sheltered feeders that can be mounted in trees or on fence posts. Hanging half coconut shells are great for suet and suet-seed mixes, although only practical for smaller birds.

Filling empty grapefruit halves with suet and seeds, or pasting up pine cones with peanut butter for hanging outside can preoccupy kids for hours. How about helping them construct a feeder from an empty milk carton? Children will be quite amazed when they actually see their creations being used by the birds. With a little imagination, very practical feeders can be constructed from the most unlikely materials. Just make sure they're safe for the birds.

An apple crate, plastic bottle and fruit basket revised into practical feeders.

HAND FEEDING

After you have been feeding the birds in your yard for a period of time, you will find that certain individuals will become accustomed to your presence. When you have established a quiet, consistent rapport with your regulars, offer them your outstretched hand with a few sunflower seeds. Before long, if your patience and calmness last, a few bolder chickadees may find the courage to land. Avoid any quick, abrupt movements while occupying their feeding grounds. Being accepted in this way is quite an honor.

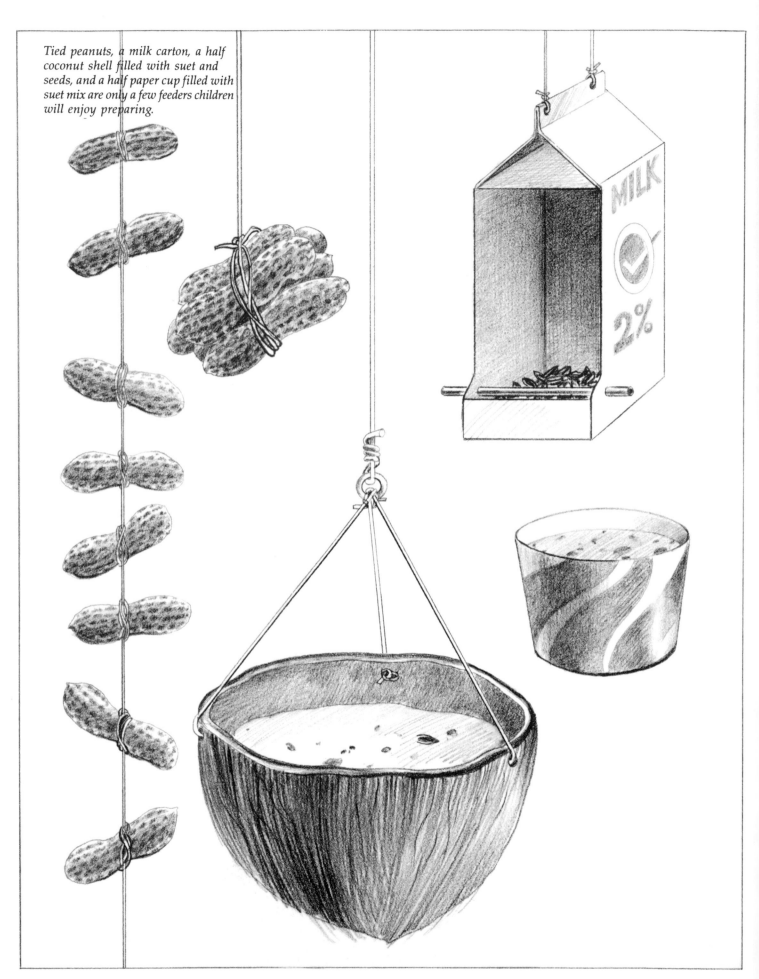

Tied peanuts, a milk carton, a half coconut shell filled with suet and seeds, and a half paper cup filled with suet mix are only a few feeders children will enjoy preparing.

Calm and patience can be rewarding.

Feeder placement

1. *Suet tied to a branch*
2. *Small hanging feeder*
3. *Double hopper-type feeder*
4. *Window shelf feeder*
5. *Hanging suet log*
6. *Railing shelf feeder*
7. *Ground table*
8. *Dried corn and sunflowers left in garden*
9. *Second-storey window shelf feeder*
10. *Raised platform feeder on fence post*

Note convenience of most feeders to back door. Also note cedar hedge and forest on far side of house serving as a natural windbreak.

5 Creating A Natural Habitat

How can you expect the birds to sing when their groves are cut down?

H. THOREAU, WALDEN

The same backyard showing shrubbery and evergreens in their second year (top), seventh year (middle) and fifteenth year (bottom). In a relatively short time it is possible to transform a barren lot into a natural garden—sheltered, private and beautiful in every season.

When the winter ground is frozen solid and covered with snow, wild birds must search the countryside far and wide in search of a few exposed berries and seeds. Many birds have come to rely on the variety of cultivated plants in our gardens as a reliable source of food and shelter. If we grow a greater assortment of trees, shrubs, flowers and food plants, we can expect to accommodate a greater number and variety of birds (even in the winter). Wherever we encourage plant life we also encourage wildlife. Even our overgrown weeds are the homes of many birds.

The ideal, natural feeding grounds for birds are those special areas where fields border forests or lawns meet shrubbery. The combination of open area for feeding and underbrush for cover seems to attract the greatest number of birds. At forest edges birds have the greatest variety of vegetation all in one small area. Most shrubs and deciduous trees after loosing their leaves still provide wind shelter, and their tangle of bare branches provide escape routes from predators. A well landscaped yard will usually provide the conditions necessary to attract birds. The yard may have clear areas of lawn at the centre, borders of flower beds and shrubs, larger trees and hedges at the perimeter. This common arrangement is practical to maintain, creates privacy and, from the point of view of the gardener, allows a good view of all the plantings. After a landscaped lot reaches some maturity, it cannot help but offer some favorable conditions for birds. Overhanging branches of shrubs and trees, tangles of flower stalks, snow-covered thickets and hedges, all provide ideal habitats for wintering birds.

When searching for food each type of bird has its own method. Juncos and sparrows peck about the areas of sheltered ground, chickadees and wrens flit through the lower branches of trees and shrubs, and nuthatches and peckers spiral the trunks of larger trees looking for insects that might be hiding in the bark. The illustration shows the various areas along a forest edge where different species might normally be found.

Fence lines bordering fields or open farmland frequently support a patchwork of wild plants where birds can search about for food. Chokecherries, pincherries, hawthorns, apples, blackberries, raspberries and wild grains are some of the plants that may be found in these areas. Fence borders

FEEDING WILD BIRDS IN WINTER

along a forest edge have even more variety. The ground in these areas are the favorite feeding spots of the Ring-necked Pheasant, Ruffed Grouse and Bobwhite. Usually the taller weeds and grasses can provide adequate cover and wind protection for these birds.

The dense foliage of evergreens such as cedar, hemlock, pine, fir and spruce provides the best winter shelter for many birds and a good food supply in the cone seeds, buds and insects to be found there. Cedar hedges in their prime have extremely dense growth, making them an excellent choice for natural borders. Ornamental evergreens, such as the many varieties of juniper available, come in all shapes and sizes, making it possible to camouflage bare walls of your house and still leave the windows exposed. Some of the lower spreading junipers become entirely snow-covered in the winter, leaving an open sheltered area under their thick berry-producing branches.

Tree nurseries carry a tremendous variety of evergreens, probably because they can provide instant landscaping, unlike other shrubs and trees whick take longer to get established. Indigenous stands of evergreens are usually found in the northern parts of northeastern America and along the Pacific coast and mountain regions.

Free standing hardwood trees such as oak, maple and beech can grow to such proportions that a single tree's umbrella of branches can shelter an entire yard. Some of the larger trees are in themselves entire habitats. Although leafless in the winter, the maze of branches or canopy can provide excellent cover for perching and ground-feeding birds. Large holes sometimes develop in the trunks of these trees, and with the help of insects the core can become a maze of homes for squirrels, woodpeckers and other birds. Most hardwoods are slow growing and hard to get established in the open. For this reason construction of any kind should come second to the preservation of these irreplaceable natural monuments.

Faster-growing varieties of maple (Norway and Crimson King) can develop into fine specimen trees with a little care. Manitoba maple is a fast-growing tree, hardy enough to grow in the prairie regions and one of the only trees large enough to provide adequate shelter in these areas from the cold winter winds. Other fast-growing trees you might consider planting include varieties of linden, ash, willow, poplar and elm.

SHRUBBERY

Shrubbery can serve a multitude of purposes. Its most common purpose is to help buildings blend into the rest of the landscape. Plants growing under or beside windows will allow you closer observation of many birds that come to them for food and shelter. Shrubbery in your yard can provide wonderful thickets for many birds to hide in while searching for berries, seeds and buds. There are indigenous shrubs that grow naturally in your area. Care should be taken to

Favorite habitats of different bird species

1. Upper branches and tree trunks:
Brown Creeper, Nuthatches, Downy Woodpecker, Pileated Woodpecker, Hairy Woodpecker

2. Sheltered woods, forest's edge:
Brown-headed Cowbird, Cardinal, Blue Jay, Purple Finch, Evening Grosbeak, Varied Thrush, Slate-colored Junco, Ruffed Grouse, Bobwhite

3. Thickets, larger weeds, lower Branches:
Purple Finch, Black-capped Chickadee, Fox Sparrow, Tufted Titmouse, American Tree Sparrow, Winter Wren

4. Evergreen:
Red Crossbill, Pine Grosbeak, White-winged Crossbill, Common Redpoll, Evening Grosbeak, Gray Jay, Ruby-crowned Kinglet, Steller's Jay, Cedar Waxwing

5. Mixed vegetation, marsh areas:
Red-winged Blackbird, Common Redpoll, Common Flicker

6. Fence lines, fields:
Common Grackle, Common Crow, Mourning Dove, Band-tailed Pigeon, Ring-necked Pheasant

7. Open ground:
Snow Bunting, Mourning Dove, Canada Goose,

8. Forest-sheltered ground:
Rufous-sided Towhee, Slate-colored junco, California Quail

encourage such growth, for the birds may find these shrubs as useful as the ornamental ones you have planted. Rather than a single trunk or stem most shrubs have many branches, which creates sheltered areas and hidden perches close to the ground level. Often thorny types of shrubs will prevent the intrusion of larger animals and birds of prey onto the feeding grounds of smaller birds.

FOOD PLANTS

A single oak tree and its maze of branches can provide shelter and food for many different birds and animals.

Any garden that you plant to feed yourself will inevitabley feed various birds as well. Certain measures may have to be taken in the summer months to prevent birds from taking all your raspberries, cherries and strawberries, but fall leftovers in your garden (plants gone to seed) can help many birds through the winter. Sunflowers, corn and beans are the types of garden leftovers that the snow will not cover up.

The following is a list of various shrubs, trees and food plants that sustain edible produce into the winter months. When landscaping a yard, you should consider planting some of the following:

PLANTS THAT HOLD THEIR FRUITS INTO THE WINTER MONTHS

Amur Cork tree
Amur Honeysuckle
Barberry
Bayberry
Common Hackberry
Coralberry
Eastern Red Cedar
European Cranberry bush
Hawthorn
Holly
Japanese Rose
Russian Olive
Sargent Crabapple
Snowberry
Staghorn Sumac
Viburnum
Winterberry

SOME SUMMER-NESTING PLANTS

Barberry
Buckthorn
Crabapple
Dogwood
Elderberry
Hawthorn
Hemlock
Holly
Mulberry
Nannyberry
Pines
Spruce

SOME PLANTS THAT ATTRACT BIRDS FOR THEIR FRUIT, SUMMER-FALL

Arrowwood
Blackberry
Blue Elder
Chokecherry
Cherry, sweet
Cotoneaster
Crabapple
Dogwood
High Bush Blueberry
High Bush Cranberry
Japanese Rose
Mountain Ash
Mulberry
Nannyberry
Pincherry
Plum
Pyracantha
Raspberry
Serviceberry
Sumac

SOME HEDGE OR SCREEN PLANTS

Barberry
Privet
Cedar
Common Lilac
Juniper
Fir
Deutzia
Holly
Yew
Hemlock

WALL CLIMBERS
(TO SCREEN WALL SURFACES, FENCES)

Clematis
Bittersweet
Eunymus
English Ivy
Boston Ivy
Virginia Creeper
Trumpet Vine

Natural windbreaks:

1. *Cedar hedge*
2. *Holly*
3. *Mixed evergreens*
4. *Privet*
5. *Valley location*
6. *Orchard*
7. *Overgrown fenceline*
8. *Mixed mature trees*

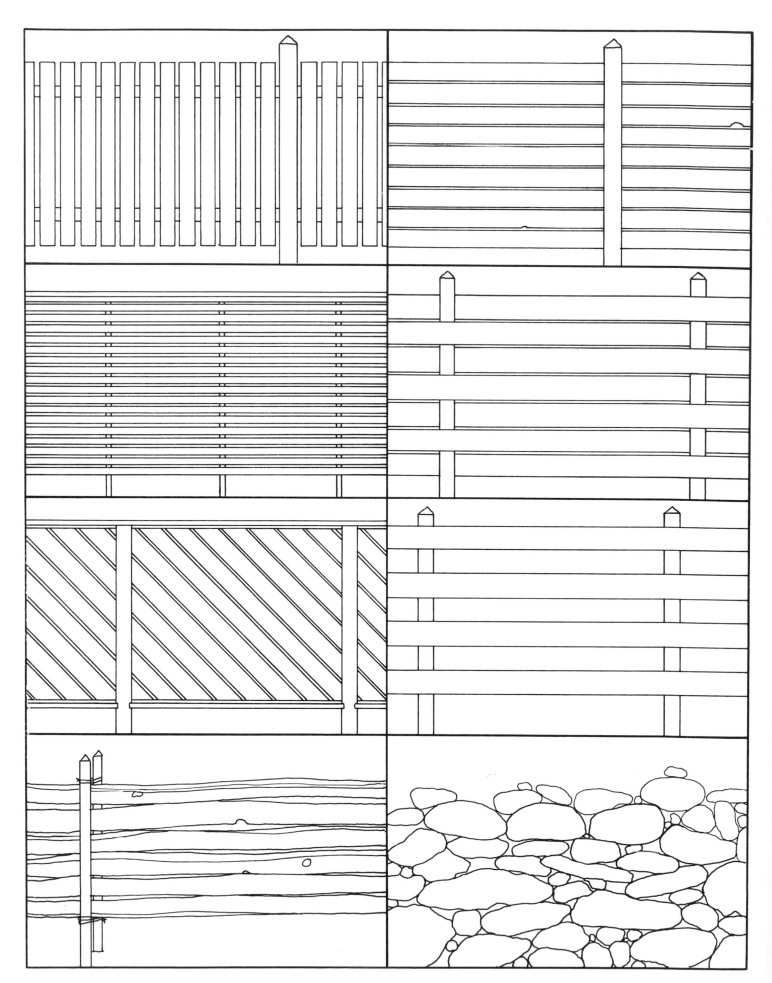

Instant windbreaks in the form of fences can suffice until shrubbery and growth take over. Illustration shows different styles appropriate for privacy and shelter.

6 Problems and Solutions

The cat comes in from an early walk amid the weeds. She is full of sparrows and wants no more breakfast this morning, unless it be a saucer of milk, the dear creature. I saw her studying ornithology between the corn rows.

H. THOREAU, WALDEN

SQUIRRELS

Most squirrels will find a way to invade any feeder, but making their approach difficult will be sufficient to keep them from dominating the feeding area.

Keeping your feeders from being emptied by greedy squirrels can be most frustrating if you have to physically chase them away every five minutes. An inverted funnel-shaped piece of aluminum or galvanized sheet metal attached to your feeding pole may keep squirrels out of your hopper-type feeders or raised platforms. Small feeders and suet bags should be hung away from branches, rooftops and trees to prevent squirrels from jumping across to them. If they are hung from the middle of a stretched wire (visible plastic-covered), approach for squirrels will be difficult. Slip a five-foot length of hosing over the wire on both sides of the hanging point. This will make balance even more difficult for squirrels.

Fasten down net-covered suet securely with twine, otherwise squirrels may run off with the whole sack.

Of all the squirrels you will find the smaller red squirrels are the most aggressive. Very few gismos will foil these squirrels for long. It is fascinating to watch them trying out their latest tactics. As long as your installations inhibit their approach, you will find it unnecessary to chase them away. Don't be too ruthless: squirrels store most of their loot, their memories are bad and before long birds find half of their caches.

Supplying squirrels with a few of their favorite foods (peanuts, suet leftovers) in a special area away from your bird feeders may also distract them long enough to allow the more reserved birds to feed.

BIRDS THAT TAKE PRIORITY

Hoping to feed only the more timid birds rather than the ever-present Starlings and House Sparrows is futile. You may be able to sidetrack some of these birds by scattering their favorite foods (bread and small seeds) on the ground away from your regular feeders. Cutting off these foods may also reduce their numbers.

Blue Jays can also be very pushy at feeders. Their raucous behavior and larger size works well to intimidate other birds. On the other hand, they are very useful in that they are the first to scream if a cat happens to arrive on the scene.

Blue Jays don't travel in great numbers like the flocks of

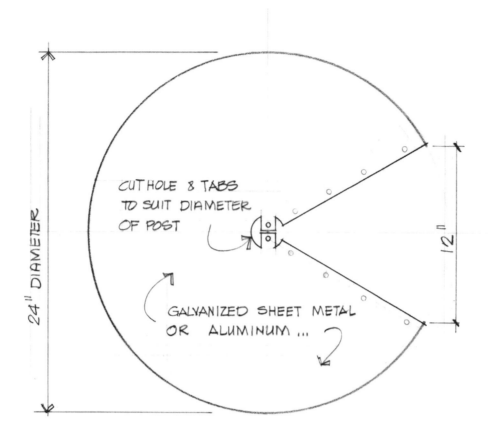

CUT HOLE & TABS
TO SUIT DIAMETER
OF POST

GALVANIZED SHEET METAL
OR ALUMINUM ...

24" DIAMETER

12"

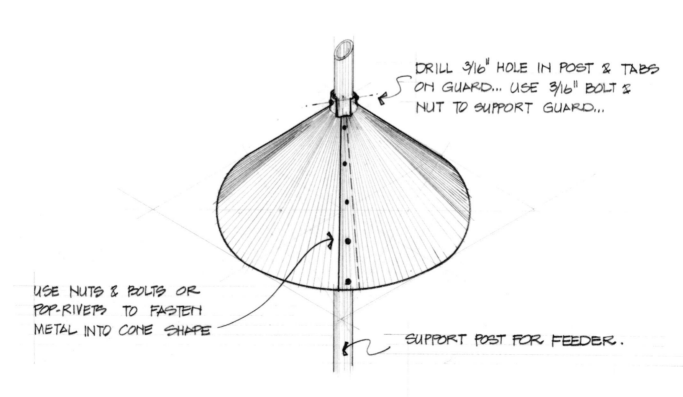

DRILL 3/16" HOLE IN POST & TABS
ON GUARD... USE 3/16" BOLT &
NUT TO SUPPORT GUARD...

USE NUTS & BOLTS OR
POP-RIVETS TO FASTEN
METAL INTO CONE SHAPE

SUPPORT POST FOR FEEDER.

OTHER SQUIRREL GUARDS

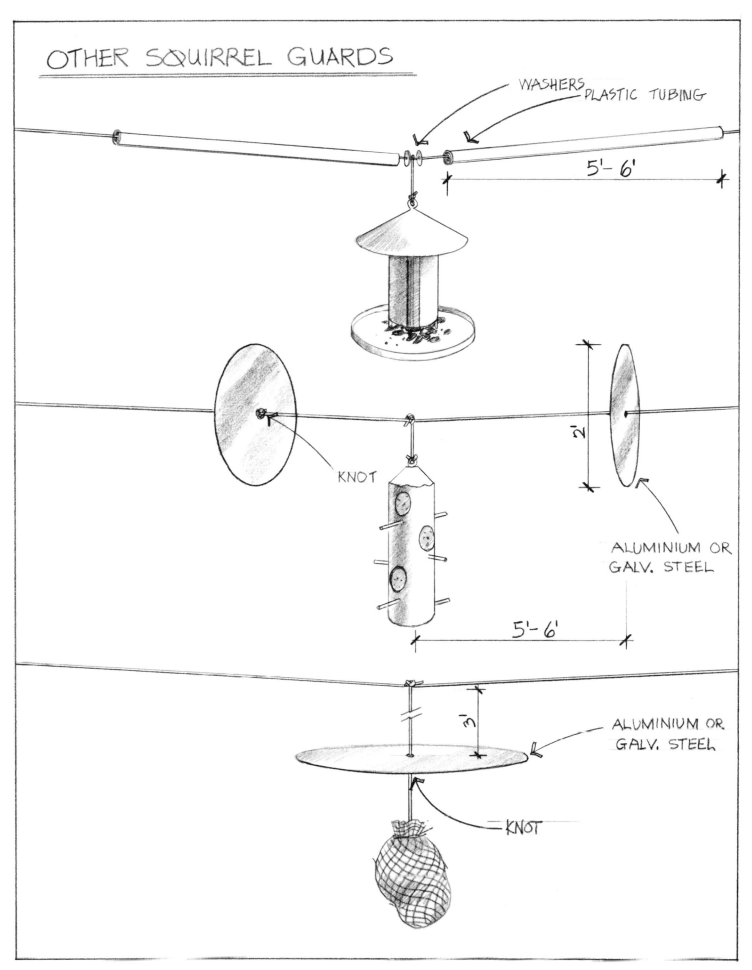

WASHERS
PLASTIC TUBING

5'- 6'

KNOT

2'

ALUMINIUM OR
GALV. STEEL

5'- 6'

3'

ALUMINIUM OR
GALV. STEEL

KNOT

Evening Grosbeaks that can arrive in the later winter. When winter has passed its coldest phase, be sure to have pounds of sunflower seeds in several other raised feeders to prevent overcrowding. Don't despair — the yellow invasion will disappear as fast as it comes.

CATS

When placing feeders or scattering feed, stay clear of extremely dense foliage and other places where cats can hide. No disciplinary action will ever change the basic nature of a cat. Your own cat should be provided with a bell. (Of course, if your cat is decimating the bird population, you shouldn't attempt yard feeding at all.)

Ground feeding close to dense foliage may be putting birds at the mercy of a waiting cat.

SPILLAGE

Any feed that may be knocked from your feeders by larger birds will be snapped up by ground-feeding birds such as juncos and sparrows. If you find abnormal amounts of feed on the ground, it may be necessary to install a higher lip around the feeding platform.

CROWDING

If your feeding area has become overcrowded, you might try installing a ground table or another hanging feeder. Expansion may be the answer. However, if most of your guests are House Sparrows and Starlings, try cutting back on bread and small seeds and temporarily stop ground feeding until their flocks have reduced to a reasonable size.

BAD WEATHER AND CRITICAL TIMES

In the early spring many birds are returning north, but some arrive a little too soon and are caught in a weather pattern of heavy snow or freezing rain. At times like these scatter a selection of feed far and wide after the storm has subsided. This will offer many more birds food, especially the shy ones or birds unfamiliar with your feeders. West coast weather can take a sudden turn for the worse anytime during the winter months, dumping a foot of wet snow in a matter of hours. Again a little extra widespread feeding will help birds until thaw.

SANITATION AND STORAGE

Store feed grains, sunflower seeds, corn, etc. in a cool, dry place, preferably in lid-covered containers (eg. plastic garbage cans). Some forms of mould in grain and corn are poisonous. Keep dry.

Keep suet refrigerated and make sure to replace old suet that may have gone rancid. Suet feeders should be in the shade. Remove old or wet feed from feeders. Periodic washing of feeders to rinse off bird waste is a good practice. AVOID FEEDING BIRDS ANYTHING SPOILED, MOULDY, RANCID OR TAINTED.

Don't litter your yard with heaps of kitchen scraps. They may rot, or you might attract some other unwanted scavengers.

BIRDS HITTING WINDOWS

Sometimes there will be so much traffic outside your windows that accidents are bound to happen. If your feeders are on the brighter side of your house, you may have fewer incidents of birds hitting windows as the sun should cause some reflection or glare. However, if you are feeding on the shady side of your house, there is the chance that birds will try to fly through a window and out the other side where perhaps they can see the landscape. Hanging sheer curtains or drawing the drapes on windows where possible can help. A piece of 10" x 4" paper fringed at the bottom and taped to the outside of the window will help prevent birds from flying through (see illustration).

If a bird strikes your window, it may only be stunned. Carefully pick the bird up in the palm of your hand. You should feel a fast pulse if the bird is alive. A flapping, **spastic** bird should be restricted with gentle hand confinement. Place stunned birds in a paper towel-lined box (shoe box) that allows ventilation. Keep the bird warm, secluded **and** calm until completely recovered. Restrict the bird's erratic movements as this will only injure it further. Release the bird in the same location you found it.

On the shaded side of a house, glare or reflection off windows will be at a minimum. If birds can see light through the house or can see the landscape on the other side, they are more apt to fly into the windows, mistaking this route for a clear passage.

A paper or foil streamer taped to the outside of the window, or sheer curtains, can help prevent accidents.

METAL

Do not use metal on feeders where birds will be landing or feeding. Their eyes and tongues may freeze if they should by chance come in contact with these cold surfaces. Also metal can have jagged edges that may cut. The use of wire for hanging is fine as long as it is clearly visible. Colored plastic-wrapped wire is the best. When building suet feeders avoid metal mesh as a means of holding suet in place. Fish net or plastic onion bag mesh is safer and easier to use.

PRESERVATIVES

Do not use preservatives on feeders as most contain nasty, poisonous compounds that kill fungus growth. Weathering turns wood an attractive silver-gray color, but if you must apply a finish use lineseed oil or spar varnish. Spar varnish should be thoroughly dry before you begin to use the feeder. Spar varnish is not poisonous and can take extreme temperatures without cracking or flaking away. Use preservatives on wood posts below ground level only.

Scatter feed far and wide when the last snow storm comes as an unwelcome surprise for many birds just back from the south.

Recommended Reading

Clement, Roland C. *The Living World of Audubon*. New York: Grosset & Dunlop, 1974.

Godfrey, W. Earl. *The Birds of Canada*. Illustrated by S.D. MacDonald. Ottawa: National Museums of Canada/National Museum of Natural Sciences, 1966.

Goodwin, Derek. *Birds of Man's World*. Ithaca, N.Y. & London: Cornell University Press & British Museum (Natural History), 1978.

Livingston, J.A. *Birds of the Eastern Forest 1*. Illustrated by J.F. Landsdowne. Toronto: McClelland & Stewart, 1968.

_____.*Birds of the Eastern Forest 2*. Illustrated by J.F. Landsdowne. Toronto: McClelland & Stewart, 1970.

_____.*Birds of the Northern Forest*. Illustrated by J.F. Landsdowne. Toronto: McClelland & Stewart, 1966.

_____.*Birds of the West Coast*. Illustrated by J.F. Landsdowne. Toronto: McClelland & Stewart, 1976.

Peterson, Roger Tory. *A Field Guide to the Birds*. Boston: Houghton Mifflin Company, 1947. This is an excellent reference for positive identification.

_____.*A Field Guide to Western Birds*. Boston: Houghton Mifflin Company, 1961.